Alcohol and Poverty in Sri Lanka

Bergljot Baklien
Diyanath Samarasinghe

Alcohol and Poverty
in
Sri Lanka

First Published 2003

© Copyright reserved
FORUT

Published by
FORUT

All rights reserved. No part of this publication may be reproduced, stored in a retrieval system or transmitted in any form or by any means, electronic, mechanical, photocopying or otherwise, without prior written permission of the authors.

ISBN 955 - 9193 - 02 - 3

Cover and Graphic design
Varuni de Silva

Printed in Sri Lanka by
SRIDEVI

Mahendra Senanayake
Sridevi Printers (Pvt) Ltd.
No. 27, Pepiliyana Road
Nedimala - Dehiwala

Table of Contents

Summary 1

1 Introduction and methodology
1.1 Introduction 9
1.2 Methodology 15
1.2.1 A qualitative approach in several field sites 15
1.2.2 Field assistants for observation and interviews 16
1.2.3 Individual information about social activities 18
1.2.4 Some experiences from the field work 19
1.2.5 Supplementary data from the urban setting 22
1.2.6 Quantitative study 23
1.2.7 Ethical considerations 24

2 Results of quantitative study
2.1 Sample 25
2.2 Alcohol use 26
2.3 Money spent on alcohol 27
2.4 Behaviour after alcohol use 28
2.5 Subjective effect of alcohol 29
2.6 Image of alcohol users 30
2.7 Comment 32

3 Urban settings, Colombo
3.1 Colombo is where everything comes together 34
3.2 Our sources 36
3.3 An overcrowded residential setting I 36
3.3.1 Environment and facilities 38
3.3.2 The people and their life style 38
3.3.3 Freedom 42
3.3.4 The economy 48

3.3.5	Alcohol and other substance use	50
3.3.6	Symbolism of alcohol	52
3.4	An overcrowded residential setting II	54
3.4.1	An example: Upali	55
3.4.2	Another example: Chandana	56
3.5	A commercial centre - Pettah	59
3.5.1	Example: Gunapala	60
3.5.2	Example: Velu and Chaminda	62
3.6	The cooperative shop	65
3.6.1	Example: Malinie	65
3.6.2	Example: Sanjeewa	67
3.6.3	The setting in general	68
3.7	Boarding life	72
3.7.1	Example: Gemunu	72
3.7.2	Example: Thusitha	73
3.8	The three-wheeler stand	77
3.8.1	Example: Jayantha	80
3.8.2	Poverty	81
3.8.3	Alcohol	81
3.8.4	Some contrasts	83
3.9	Places of entertainment and leisure	84
3.9.1	Hotels	84
3.9.2	The shopping mall	86
3.9.3	Other leisure settings	90
3.9.4	Role models and others of influence	92
3.10	Poor lives in Colombo – final impressions	93
3.10.1	Lives of the economically deprived in Colombo	94
3.10.2	'Porosity'	94
3.10.3	'Jealousy'	94
3.10.4	'Powerful individuals'	95
3.10.5	Alcohol and other substance use	96

4   Rural settings: poverty and alcohol use

4.1	Dry zone: poverty and vulnerability	100
4.1.1	The dry zone villages	100
4.1.2	Poverty, indebtedness and gambling in the dry zone	102
4.2	Wet zone, closer to Colombo	104
4.2.1	The wet zone village	104

4.2.2	Poverty and economy in the wet zone village	106
4.3	A fishing community	106
4.3.1	The fishing village in Gampaha	106
4.3.2	Poverty and economy in the fishing community	108
4.4	The estate community	112
4.4.1	The tea estate	112
4.4.2	Poverty and economy among the estate workers	114
4.5	Communities of displaced persons	115
4.5.1	The village in Vavuniya	115
4.5.2	Poverty and economy of those displaced in Vavuniya	116
4.5.3	A village of displaced persons in Puttalam	118
4.5.4	Poverty and economy of those displaced in Puttalam	119
4.6	Conspicuous consumption, envy and jealousy	122
4.7	Alcohol consumption as a part of everyday life	124
4.8	Alcohol consumption on special occasions	128
4.9	Norms about drinking and alcohol use	129
4.9.1	Excuses of people drinking	129
4.9.2	Drunken behaviour	130
4.9.3	Norms surrounding alcohol consumption	131
4.10	Economic consequences of alcohol use	133
4.11	Social consequences of alcohol use	134
4.12	Domestic violence	137
4.12.1	A case story from Vavuniya	137
4.12.2	High prevalence of domestic violence	137
4.12.3	Violence and masculinity	138
4.12.4	Norms about non interference	139
4.12.5	Alcohol and violence	141

5   Conclusions

5.1	Alcohol	143
5.1.1	The role of alcohol	143
5.1.2	Money spent on alcohol	144
5.1.3	The role of alcohol in making the socially unacceptable acceptable	145
5.1.4	The subjective effect of alcohol	146
5.1.5	'Fun' and illicit alcohol	147
5.2	Poverty	147
5.2.1	Dimensions of poverty	147

5.2.2	Envy and jealousy	149
5.2.3	Active obstruction of others' development	149
5.3	Poverty versus low income	151
5.4	Potential for change	152
5.5	Alcohol, poverty and development	153
5.5.1	Ambiguous norms	153
5.5.2	The paradoxical role of alcohol in the development process	155
	Glosssary	156
	References	157

List of Photographs - Colombo

		Contributor	Page
1.	Birds eye view of Colombo city	Prasanna Hennayake	34-35
2.	Colombo's busy streets 1	Duminda Gamage	37
3.	Pavements	Duminda Gamage	37
4.	Bus stand 1	Duminda Gamage	39
5.	Rush hour	Varuni de Silva	39
6.	Garbage mountain	Garvis Alfredson	41
7.	By the rail track	Duminda Gamage	43
8.	Life in overcrowded areas	Alfredson	43
9.	Hot tin roof	Garvis Alfredson	45
10.	Clothes dryer	Garvis Alfredson	45
11.	Factory workers	Prasanna Hennayake	49
12.	Coconut plucker	Varuni de Silva	49
13.	Construction worker	Varuni de Silva	49
14.	Municipal worker	Varuni de Silva	51
15.	Vegetable seller	Duminda Gamage	51
16.	Cement block house	Duminda Gamage	54
17.	Attached housing	Rasitha Perera	56
18.	By the tap	Garvis Alfredson	57
19.	Fort railway station	Varuni de Silva	61
20.	Bus stand 2	Duminda Gamage	61
21.	Night life 1	Duminda Gamage	63
22.	Night life 2	Duminda Gamage	63
23.	Bar	Prasanna Hennayake	69
24.	Wedding	Duminda Gamage	69
25.	Boarding house	Duminda Gamage	75
26.	Machine operator	Varuni de Silva	75
27.	Three wheeler on Galle road	Varuni de Silva	79
28.	Three wheeler stand	Varuni de Silva	79
29.	Bar 2	Prasanna Hennayake	85
30.	Chinese restaurant	Varuni de Silva	85
31.	Majestic city	Duminda Gamage	89
32.	Majestic city inside	Duminda Gamage	89
33.	Galle face	Varuni de Silva	91
34.	Enjoying the sea breeze	Varuni de Silva	91

List of Photographs - Rural Settings

	Photographer	Page
35. Vegetables for sale	Prasanna Hennayake	98
36. Village life	Prasanna Hennayake	98
37. Boat on Wewa	Duminda Gamage	99
38. Elephants bathing	Varuni de Silva	99
39. Drawing water for farming	Duminda Gamage	101
40. Drying chillies	Duminda Gamage	101
41. Harvesting	Varuni de Silva	103
42. Hay stack	Varuni de Silva	103
43. Rubber estate	Raveen Hanwella	105
44. Rubber tapping	Raveen Hanwella	105
45. Collecting tapped rubber	Raveen Hanwella	107
46. Rubber transported to factory	Raveen Hanwella	107
47. Fishing village	Duminda Gamage	109
48. Fishing boat	Duminda Gamage	109
49. Unloading the catch	Duminda Gamage	111
50. Auction on the beach	Duminda Gamage	111
51. Tea estate	Garvis Alfredson	113
52. Tea plucker	Garvis Alfredson	113
53. Camp for displaced persons	Varuni de Silva	117
54. Displaced and nothing to do	Prasanna Hennayake	117
55. Fruit seller	Duminda Gamage	121
56. Cleaning up time	Duminda Gamage	121
57. Farmer wanting to be photographed	Duminda Gamage	125
58. Swimming pool	Duminda Gamage	135
59. Travellers	Raveen Hanwella	135

Foreword

This report *Alcohol and poverty in Sri Lanka* is the result of an assignment from FORUT Norway's Local Action Against Alcohol and Drugs campaign to the Norwegian institute for rural and urban research (NIBR). The research project started in June 2002 and was finished in July 2003.

The project has been carried out as a cooperation by Bergljot Baklien, senior researcher NIBR and Dr. Diyanath Samarasinghe, University of Colombo, Sri Lanka. Baklien has been the project leader, and has done the project planning and the shaping of the project. In the reporting, Baklien has been responsible for chapter 4 on rural settings, and Samarasinghe has written chapter 2 analyzing the quantitative data and chapter 3 about the urban setting. Chapters 1 and 5 are a joint responsibility. The authors share the responsibility for the total product presented here.

We would like to thank Øystein Bakke at FORUT for the trust placed in us, our field coordinators Duminda Guruge and Rashan Haniffa, and all our field assistants. We are also grateful to all those informants who willingly told us about their lives. The cooperation received was almost total. Thanks also go to all of the staff of FORUT, Sri Lanka and of the Foundation for Health Promotion who facilitated the tasks of administering the study. In the last phase of the project Varuni de Silva did splendid work in making the most attractive and readable product possible within the budget available.

Sidsel Sverdrup
Research director NIBR

Summary

This report is on a study of 'Alcohol and Poverty' commissioned by the development agency FORUT (Norway). The study ran from June 2002 to June 2003. It covered several settings specified by FORUT, as the agency commissioning the study. These settings included urban overcrowded communities (commonly referred to as 'slums'), dry zone and wet zone rural communities, an estate sector community and a setting of persons internally displaced. To provide better coverage, a predominantly Roman Catholic 'fishing' community was added to the list originally provided.

Methodology

The methodology was principally an in-depth qualitative inquiry through trained and regularly supervised field assistants. The in-depth component required the field assistant to be in the given community for a period of at least ten days. There were seven locations so studied. This was supplemented by a brief inquiry in three other settings to obtain greater coverage. An 'informal' entry was used to study eight other urban settings within the capital Colombo.

In addition, a short questionnaire exploring quantitatively some variables connected to alcohol use was administered at the end of the qualitative study.

Principal findings

Poverty

'Poverty' could refer to many things, including a limitation in richness of people's lives, poor income or lack of basic needs. All of these, unsurprisingly, went together in most of the settings that we studied. Lives were limited in the range of things to be involved in or to do, in variety of interests, in aspirations to aim for and in comforts and range of opportunities to enjoy leisure. We found that people with poor income generally, but not always, had poorer or more limited lives. But poverty of lives was not always a function of poor income.

Poverty seemed strongly to imply uncertainty and a lack of control over the future. Many had such regular and routine lives, with so little variation, that they could forecast today the routine they would have to follow on any given day in the future, even ten years hence. But such persons too still felt uncertain about the future. They were still at the mercy of such things as droughts and other natural disasters. Any possible variation from a routine and unchanging life could occur only due to a calamity!

Among the economically deprived there was a great deal of intra-group differences. The poor are of many levels, but some common features that were evident are listed below.

Porosity

Many of the most poor in the city are crowded together. Much of the character of their lives stems from being unable to 'wall themselves off', for example as a family, from what happens in their community. Most of the poor in the village and the not-so-poor in the city have a slightly better defined space, a boundary. But porosity is found in rural settings too, particularly among those living in 'camps' for the internally displaced, the estate workers living in the line houses, and in the fishing community.

Because of not having a boundary beyond which the rest of the world or community cannot intrude (or 'porosity' of the living space), the poor in the city's overcrowded tenements find it difficult to improve economically. Especially so if others around them do not particularly want them to. This phenomenon has major implications for those living in such circumstances and for those working for development in such settings.

Porosity has other important consequences too. The lack of private space makes it difficult to resolve conflicts in private. 'Loss of face' has to be avoided and, strangely, there is probably more fighting and aggression where people cannot have a boundary between themselves and the rest of the world. Or the fighting is more visible.

Envy and jealousy

A feeling of 'envy' for anybody who rises above the rest was strongly evident. Whether this tendency, to want to keep all others no better than oneself, is a feature outside this kind of community has to be studied. But it certainly is a strong element in these communities. Many of our informants have referred to this as 'jealousy'. This tendency is most evident in relation to money and material possessions, and was common to both rural and urban settings.

More subtle improvements are envied too. A couple that is happy together will be envied. There may even be attempts to impede their wellbeing. A man who does not consume alcohol daily with the crowd can be targeted in the same way.

Visible consumption

People spend money on things that give them social credit. We found that there are massive expenditures on alcohol for 'celebrations' in poor families. It is almost as if they want to be envied their expenditure. At the same time as they complain of others wanting to keep them down because of envy or 'jealousy' there is a desire to do exactly the things that make other people envy them. Show off is a kind of must. The need to be envied, or to get social credit, is probably an important factor that keeps people poor. Families getting into debt, and having to pay interest of over ten per cent per month for life, was reportedly common following even a single celebration such as that for a daughter reaching menarche.

Lack of control

Poor people seemed to have more direct pressure applied on them than the rich, regarding how they should live. Others in the community could directly demand conformity. This applies even to how they choose to conduct a 'private' event.

Parents, in a poor community, who did not wish to have a party when their daughter reached menarche, could be asked to explain why. Some informants said that they could even be forced to change their decision.

Criminality

Criminal acts and violence appeared rather close to the surface in the poorest communities. Whether similar degrees of violence and criminality in richer communities are somehow hidden requires separate investigation. But the overall impression was that violent and aggressive behaviour was always lurking somewhere close to the surface. And it was as if this tendency strongly influenced life in the poorest communities. 'Everybody' recognized, for example, that the trade in illicit drugs and illicit alcohol should not be seriously challenged. The undertone of possible organized criminal elements was more evident in the urban settings.

'Impossibility' of overcoming poverty

A repeated theme was that people could never emerge from poverty as long as they lived in their overcrowded urban setting, irrespective of the income they were able to earn. One factor underlying this is the 'porosity' of living arrangements that we referred to earlier. There is no room for gradual growth or development. Any progress is visible, and others are not keen to see just one family prosper. The sense was that others would not allow people to develop, and that the shared lives allow them to obstruct those who want to develop. There may be other barriers too, common to both rural and urban settings. One of these is that people have not only to overcome their own personal and private poverty. They have to overcome the culture of poverty that is a part of their surroundings and their everyday life. It appears that acceptance of current circumstances is more adaptive than trying to overcome them.

Alcohol and other substance use

Significant heroin use was almost entirely an urban phenomenon. Cannabis smoking was common in several rural settings. Alcohol was nearly everywhere. Alcohol and heroin are needed as an essential daily commodity by a significant minority of the poor in urban communities. Alcohol, mostly illicit, is similarly needed daily by a significant minority of the rural. Tobacco is too, but it is somehow less noticed or commented upon. Alcohol and heroin get much more attention than tobacco does.

An apparent discrepancy was found between the qualitative and quantitative study results. In the quantitative study 63 % reported that they never consumed alcohol. Only 17 % consumed more often than once a week. But the qualitative study yielded the impression that nearly every male wanted to have alcohol at weddings and celebrations and they would all protest openly about not being able to enjoy the event if there was no alcohol. But in the anonymous quantitative study just 32% said that the act of drinking was a pleasant experience while only 14% said that the experience of 'being drunk' was pleasant.

The data were analysed separately and could not be clarified with the respondents. There are several possible explanations for this seeming contradiction. One of these is that, during social events, a minority of very vociferous individuals who want to promote alcohol are able to create an impression that becomes somehow the view of the whole group, most of whom remain silent.

Perceptions of 'alcohol user' and 'abstainer'

The quantitative component of this study included a focus on how people saw alcohol use and users. In this, fifty nine percent of the total number of respondents rated alcohol users as less attractive than others (versus 20 % who found them more attractive). Similar ratings were obtained for whether alcohol users were seen as stronger or weaker than the others, more or less intelligent than others and whether they enjoyed life more or less than others.

On nearly all of these parameters the occasional drinkers and abstainers had close to identical proportions holding the same opinion, quite different from the proportions given by frequent (twice a week or more) drinkers. The classification of people into 'alcohol users' and 'abstainers' is often used in Sri Lanka. This division may be artificial. The more 'natural' division appears to be between the occasional users and non-users on the one side and the frequent users on the other.

Cost of alcohol

The effect of alcohol on the community was enormous. It was not just the money spent on alcohol, but also its impact on norms of behaviour. But the monetary cost too was high. The findings of our quantitative study correspond to what has generally been known and reported about the monetary expenditures on alcohol. Over 10 % of male respondents report spending as much as (or more than!) their regular income on alcohol. An additional number probably comes close to this. From a community development perspective this is a frighteningly large group – as they are probably the most abjectly poor and the most difficult to help.

In our qualitative study we discovered that 'calculation' of the expenditure on alcohol grossly underestimates the real cost. And this is not only because of people deliberately or unwittingly 'underestimating' the amount of money they spend on alcohol. There are two other mechanisms which came to light.

One of these is that heavier drinkers make others pay for their alcohol using a variety of tactics. And this expenditure is not registered either by those who consume the subsidized alcohol or by those who subsidize it. There are several means through which others are made to pay for part of the alcohol expenditures of the regular or heavier users. Heavier consumers ensure, for example, that every 'fun' occasion is made into an alcohol occasion. The feeling that much alcohol must be served for a 'proper' party or occasion is constantly reiterated. People who are new to a group or junior in a workplace or boarding are made to take up much of the bill for alcohol when they go out with heavier drinking seniors. Collecting money from light alcohol users and non-users too, when special events are organized is common.

The second mechanism through which some alcohol expenditures became invisible was the inattention to the amount spent during special occasions. Weddings, 'big girl parties' and other celebrations called for large expenditures. The heavy alcohol component of this was not included in calculations of 'average' alcohol expenditures. But this money was considerable. People reported becoming indebted, and having to pay high rates of interest to 'loan sharks', sometimes for life. Property, jewellery and other possessions were reported to be lost to the family in this way.

Behaviour and alcohol use

People in the settings studied appeared to be allowed freely to transgress personal boundaries after consuming alcohol. This was probably more evident than in 'wealthier' settings. Those who wanted to control what others say, do and think were able, in the drinking setting, to tell them forcibly what they should do. The stronger person, during the drinking event, was given the right to comment and criticize the conduct of others in the community. Some informants claimed that people said to be 'jealous' used this opportunity to ensure that others didn't surpass them.

Domestic violence and gender based violence was almost taken for granted in nearly all settings as an 'automatic' consequence of alcohol use. Deprivation of the needs of children due to the father's heavy alcohol use was regarded simply as a misfortune of the children concerned, and not a matter for special concern or mention. Women being abused in the home by 'drunken' husbands was known, and even heard, but it was accepted as fate or as an evil caused by alcohol.

Striking differences too were visible in the way that alcohol affects behaviour. In an urban hotel, a wealthier group consuming alcohol behaved very differently from a group of poorer workers who came there once to drink as a special treat. Only the poorer drinkers became noisy and conspicuous. Similarly, when alcohol was used surreptitiously in places where it was prohibited, people did not become loud and aggressive.

Alcohol and public norms

Many informants highlighted the impact of alcohol on public norms. The 'license' afforded by alcohol to say and do things without too much concern about social consequences has consequences. It allows the physically strong or aggressive to dominate others. And it permits 'unacceptable' behaviour to be openly admitted. Previously unacceptable behaviour that people learn to brag about in drinking settings was said to become gradually more socially acceptable with time. These ceased to cause shame or embarrassment, even in non-drinking settings, after they were publicly boasted about while intoxicated.

There are norms about alcohol drinking too. It is almost shameful, for instance, to drink kasippu publicly, but it is not so shameful to be seen drunk on kasippu. Another example is the creation of strong norms commanding people to serve alcohol on special celebratory occasions.

Main conclusions and recommendations

There are a great variety of meanings attached to alcohol use. So also of behaviours related to use and reported subjective experiences with alcohol. Understanding these provides potential for interventions to reduce harmful consequences of alcohol use.

Whilst alcohol remains a great hindrance to development for the poor, some forms of alcohol use are celebrated as the very symbol of economic success. In the wealthier world the alcohol arena is one in which the search for a modern identity is acted out. How this influences the consumption and images within the poor world should be recognised, as also other unseen sequelae of modernisation.

Money spent on alcohol by poor families and communities is underestimated to a remarkable degree. This is not due simply to deliberate or unwitting under-reporting. A large part of alcohol expenditure is unseen. One reason is that others 'subsidise' a significant part of the alcohol used by heavy or regular drinkers, which neither party notices or reports. A second is that the sometimes huge and unbearable cost of alcohol for celebrations or events is not reported. Lifelong debt and misery too often follows just one family event. Another alcohol expenditure, unrecognised and unreported, is 'unexpected' money or illegally earned money being immediately 'busted' on alcohol. A cultural change is needed to make these expenses evident and to help communities address the social assumptions that lead to such expenses.

A large proportion of the poor is heavily into regular alcohol use – and an additional number in the city into heroin use as well. Families in these categories are likely to be the most abjectly poor and most in need of 'development'. They are also likely to be the most resistant and difficult to help progress. The risk that the most in need will be left out of, or fail to benefit from, all poverty alleviation or developmental endeavours is high indeed. Special, focussed, attention to this group of heavy alcohol and other drug users is essential if community development efforts are not to miss the most deprived.

Freedom from normal social norms when 'intoxicated' allows much abuse of weaker members of society, especially women. Children too are open to abuse in this way but the reports were mostly of women being abused. The 'authority' given to domineering individuals, to force others to conform by using alcohol-related aggressiveness, is used in other ways too. One such use is to forcibly prevent members of the community from improving economically. Attempts to help the poorer families to overcome their poverty have to address this 'forcible' retention in poverty, partly through force exerted under the guise of intoxication.

Acceptance and 'social cleansing' of socially disapproved behaviours occurs through these being openly proclaimed in the drinking setting. The impact of this goes beyond the drinking setting. When people are allowed to get away with boasting about breaking certain social norms, even whilst 'drunk', these norms gradually disappear.

Illicit alcohol use is rife, but its consumption is not associated with 'fun' and 'enjoyment'. This is probably just as well. But the finding should be helpful in educating people about the social modulation of alcohol effects.

Poverty has many expressions. In the worst instances, it is associated with hopeless apathy. This was particularly visible among those who had been displaced.

Envy or 'jealousy' and a tendency for communities to obstruct, actively and deliberately, the possible economic development of their neighbours are reported to be widespread. Those who don't want others to progress use subtle coercion and extortion, often under cover of 'alcohol-induced' criticisms or veiled threats. Many in overcrowded tenements believe they can never uplift themselves whilst resident there. The implications for development are that these social dynamics need to be addressed in a collective developmental effort or that people have to be provided avenues to escape the setting or its culture.

Families with much lower income than those in a 'poor' or under-serviced tenement enjoyed a better standard of living when they were resident in a different setting. This was associated with the adoption of more 'middle class' norms and aspirations. Much can learnt about the interaction of low income with other factors in generating 'poverty', by studying the relative wellbeing of low-income earners who do not belong to a 'poor culture'.

Introduction and methodology

Introduction

What is the role of alcohol in different social settings in Sri Lanka? To what extent does alcohol contribute to creating, perpetuating or worsening poverty, and to what extent is alcohol a hindrance to development? The main intention of the study reported here, is to try to address questions such as these.

In answering these questions, we shall describe every day life in different social settings in Sri Lanka, settings that seem to have only one aspect in common, poverty. We shall describe urban settings, in the so called slum communities and other localities of Colombo. In rural areas, we shall describe the situation in several agricultural villages, both in the dry zone and the wet zone, scattered over the country. We also report the situation in a fishing village, a tea estate, and settlements of internally displaced persons.

The villages are not chosen on basis of their position on any kind of poverty index. As far as we know, no such index exists. The villages are selected to cover different social settings, different parts of the country and different ethnic and religious groups. Due to limited resources, one criterion added was that it should be possible for our field assistants to visit and to stay there for ten days.

Even though the main interests of our study were alcohol and poverty, the approach in the villages was to study the everyday life of the people who lived there. Through their stories came also their descriptions of poverty, and of how they coped with their situations. The focus on everyday life also functioned to reveal what we could call the poverty culture of these villages. Anthony Giddens has pointed out how people are 'products' of a culture, which they also constantly 'reproduce' as well as change. People are shaped by their culture, but they also influence and shape their culture (Giddens 1984). One important intention of our study is to describe how this happens and the extent to which people have the capability to 'shape their culture', or maybe to escape it.

In this study we look at what could be called two cultural elements, two elements that interact strongly with each other. One is the poverty culture already mentioned, which also includes people's coping strategies and their handling of their situation. The other is the alcohol culture - how people behave when they drink and the norms and the attitudes that surround different drinking situations.

The cultural approach recognises the importance of the relations between drinking and daily life, and of the normative structures relating to drinking, in understanding differences in drinking practices and in rates of problems related to drinking (cf. Room 2002:81). Our discussion of the cultural status or role of drinking is also related to the tendency in the ethnographic literature to interpret differences in drunken comportment as cultural differences. One of the basic studies here was done by MacAndrew and Edgerton in 1969. The authors argued that cultures differ greatly in the extent to which drunkenness results in "drunken changes-for-the-worse", i.e. violent and other deviant behaviour. Implicit in MacAndrew and Edgerton's discussion was a continuum, with societies in which drunken behaviour did not differ at all from sober behaviour at one end, and societies in which serious violence was expected and seen at the other end (cf. Room 2001).

In many cultures drunkenness is used as an excuse for behaviour that is otherwise disapproved of in society, and which is normally controlled in most social contexts (Rossow 1999). But the extent to which this happens and the manner in which it occurs can vary between settings. This is to be expected even today despite the greater unification of cultures across the globe, evident even during the short span since Mac Andrew and Edgerton published their findings.

In our study we look at the norms and the attitudes regarding drunken behaviour in different social settings. We show how these norms become visible through the behaviour of those who drink, through the way they talk about their drinking, and in the way non-drinkers act towards drinking and drunken behaviour.

An overall intention of our study is to show the role of alcohol in everyday life in deprived settings. As a background we also describe these settings, and how the insecure income sources of poor people influence their life style and their coping strategies.

The concept of poverty is also an important focus for us. There are many definitions of poverty. As Dale (2000:26) spells out, the term can be used in a fairly specific and narrow sense or with wider connotations. In its narrow sense, it is usually taken to denote the basic material conditions of households in terms of

- Few and simple assets (for production and consumption)
- Low income (in cash or in kind)
- Low consumption

Households with these characteristics commonly have a problem with the regularity of supply of income and food as well. Dale (op.cit.) therefore also incorporates:
- Variable supply of cash and food

In national and international statistics on poverty, the emphasis is usually on income and consumption. In Sri Lanka, the Central Bank (1987) defines poverty as the lack of income to buy the basic minimum of food caloric energy . Based on what Yapa (1998)calls a substantive approach to poverty, we would expect that scarcity and insecurity regarding the supply of cash and food to be associated. Unemployment or underemployment is a common element or association of poverty. Kliksberg (1997) states, "prolonged unemployment leads to....increased apathy, a serious loss of interest in socialising and a gradual withdrawal from the labour force. Loss of self-esteem is a defining element." This too we should expect to find among our informants, particularly among the youngest. A study of Sri Lankan youth showed very high rates of unemployment:

Introduction and Methodology

59 % in the 15-19 age group, 50 % in the 20-25 group, and 26 % in the 26-29 group. The overall rate for youth unemployment according to a recent survey was 50 % (Lakshman 2000:62).

Concepts of absolute and relative poverty are commonly used in literature about social welfare in Western countries. In the West, the number whose basic needs are not met is small, but the share of relative poverty can be large and give rise to concern. In Sri Lanka too, and in the social settings that we have data from, the difference between absolute and relative poverty is relevant in understanding the context. The descriptions below are based on Dale (2000:28).

Absolute poverty means that the minimum material requirements for sustaining a decent life are not fulfilled; in other words basic material needs are not met. The usual question posed is whether a household has sufficient income to purchase a "basket" of basic commodities for consumption, or alternatively, produces these commodities itself. The level at which basic material needs are considered to be just met, is commonly referred to as the poverty line. Poor people are those who fall below that line.

Relative poverty denotes the material living conditions of individuals or households in a society compared to the condition of other individuals or households in that society or compared to some subjective judgement of what is "adequate". Thus the relative poverty line for households in a country may be set at one half of the average income of households in that country.

The terms absolute and relative poverty draws attention to the social and the cultural context of poor people. People living in a context where everybody else has the same low income and faces the same problems arising from low consumption and few assets, will probably experience their situation differently from such people living in a more heterogeneous context. Some persons with even a higher income and more available cash may still be constantly reminded that they have less than others in the same social setting or in social settings close to them. Sri Lankan society has big and visible income disparities and highly unequal salary structures. Unskilled workers get subsistence wages while those high in management are given much higher salaries and incentives.

It may sometimes be useful to draw a line between subjective and objective poverty. Some people are poor in the narrow meaning of the word – their existence is below the poverty line. However we met people who insist that they are poor, or even the poorest of the poor, when they clearly have sufficient food, clothing and shelter[1]. Poverty is not only a question of income. Just as important are the local norms or attitudes and the culture and its influence on the way people spend their meagre incomes. We should look also at how poverty is also a question of social capital[2].

We spoke to development workers and other officers who explained this by arguing that it can be profitable for villagers to be defined as poor. We had heard stories about families who do not mend their roof because a new or improved roof would be a visible proof that they are not so poor, and that would mean that they would lose their Samurdhi benefit. This can be regarded as a strategic action. Of course we do not know whether such ideas are widespread, or whether this is just a rumour that exists among such officers and development workers. In "our" social settings we looked for indicators not only on objective and absolute poverty, but also on relative and subjective poverty, and examined how they are related to alcohol consumption.

Identification of one's household as poor, can also be viewed in the light of theories of relative deprivation. Deprivation is felt when people compare themselves with others and believe that they should have as much as those others have. Sociology texts refer similarly to the situation of women's liberationists who compare the situation of women to men, and to African Americans who are aware that they receive less income than whites with a comparable educational background[3]. There is no absolute standard for comparison, only the conviction among certain people that they have less than some specific others have. Some of these convictions influence the self-perception and coping strategies of poorer people.

Poverty is therefore not simply a matter of low income. As Hettige (1995:27) points out, social and cultural traditions prevailing in a country may create conditions of poverty even in households with one person or more gainfully employed and earning a reasonably high income. Hettige refers to the widespread tendency of sharing resources among family members and close kin. For instance, in the absence of comprehensive income support schemes such as unemployment benefit, child endowments and old age pensions, the burden of the young and old dependants fall on the employed members of the family. The result of such dependency is that even an income which is adequate to provide a decent standard of living for those who earn it, is no defence against poverty because it is spread too thinly among a large number of persons. While such a social practice prevents starvation and total neglect of the vulnerable groups such as the aged, the disabled and the unemployed, it also ensures that nobody rises above a bare minimum existence, argues Hettige. As a consequence, where there is a strong tradition of sharing and caring, it is not only those who have no access to income sources of their own who suffer from poverty, but also those who are gainfully employed. Such a pervasive social practice acts as a form of social insurance against widespread neglect and abandonment of the weak and the vulnerable. But it may also produce negative outcomes such as the discouragement of individual initiative and enterprise, the shirking of state responsibility towards those so dependent and the reinforcement of subsistence orientation.

Hettige describes the sharing and caring as something positive, as an indication of poor people's tendency to help each other. But this normative structure can also function as a mechanism that keeps people down, and prevents them from escaping their poor living conditions.

What appears through the studies of poverty that we have referred to so far, is a complex picture. Poverty is not just one thing. A more comprehensive approach should not only cover economic and material poverty, but also several kinds of social poverty. This is particularly important when the intention is to examine how alcohol consumption and poverty are connected. Of course, "everybody" knows that there is a strong connection between alcohol and poverty. The important question for us to answer is how and to what extent alcohol contributes to poverty. This must be connected to the social functions of alcohol in different groups and to what could be called different poverty cultures.

We also focus on the availability of alcohol in different contexts, legal and illegal. Various sources claim that 50 – 70 % of the alcohol consumed is illicit. Similar numbers are given in a study by R. Abeyasinghe, who finds that 60 % of the alcohol consumed in a slum area in Colombo, is illicit (Abeyasinghe 2002:125).

The main focus of our study too is not numbers but the "thicker" descriptions of the social constructions of alcohol, and the consequences of alcohol use. As Skjelmerud reports, in her study from Namibia, alcohol consumption is given different, and rather contradictory, meanings (Skjelmerud 1999:2). One is the meaning of togetherness – drinking brings people together in an ad hoc fellowship. Another is the symbol of difference, of class – drinking is used to mark distinction. Skjelmerud shows how different aspects give a vertical and a horizontal dimension of the meanings of alcohol, as it serves to integrate as well as to separate people. Based on the drinking patterns that we identify, the meanings people ascribe to alcohol can be linked to status along the vertical and horizontal dimensions.

On the vertical dimension inequality, power relations, social mobility, and ambition can be considered. Vertically, alcohol may be related to both power and powerlessness.

To drink, and to get drunk, may be rights reserved for certain groups. Alcohol may indicate suppression. Disobedience and resistance may also be communicated through drinking. Alcohol can serve as a separation, as a marker of class and superiority. Where there are possibilities of upward social mobility, alcohol may be a way of expressing ambitions of social climbing.

On the horizontal dimension, a person's status can be linked to roles, group membership, communality, and sense of belonging. Horizontally alcohol often functions as a tool in creating a place of communality, of solidarity, where social differences are wiped out.

Drinking can be seen as a response to external influences, as well as to personal priorities and aspirations (cf. Skjelmerud 1999:19). Alcohol can be seen as a case study for social positioning and carrying out different social scripts. What different people seek in life may be reflected in their relationship to alcohol drinking, and in the symbols and meanings they ascribe to drinking. Alcohol can be seen as a symbol, which gives meaning to how people construct their realities.

In our study we follow up this approach when we ask questions about how alcohol consumption is connected to or incorporated into the poverty culture. After this introduction there is a chapter on research methodology, where we describe how data were collected. This chapter should answer the question 'How do we know?' Chapter 2 gives the findings from the urban setting, where we have data from so-called slum areas and from less deprived settings in the city. Chapter 3 describes the situation in rural settings, from the dry zone, which is characterized by poverty and vulnerability, the wet zone which is less vulnerable, the fishing community with mainly Roman Catholic inhabitants, the tea estate with Tamil workers, and two rather different communities of displaced persons.

As a part of our study we also conducted a brief survey. The results and the quantitative analysis are given in chapter 4. The last chapter concludes, places our findings in a theoretical context and relates them to other findings in the field.

Notes

1. Based on B. Baklien's experience from field work in Moneragala in connection with another research project.

2. For a discussion of the concept of social capital, see Johnston and Percy-Smith 2003.

3. Cf for ex Shephard, Jon M. (1990).

Methodology

1.2.1 A qualitative approach in several field sites

The study uses a combination of data sources and methods. The main method, however, is qualitative. Qualitative methods are more appropriate when the intention is to bring out the perspectives and constructions of the informants.

Qualitative methods are generally based on two kinds of data collection:
> In-depth, open-ended interviews. Data will consist of direct quotations from people about their experiences, opinions, feelings, and knowledge.
> Direct observations. Data will consist of detailed descriptions of people's activities, behaviours, actions, and the full range of interpersonal interactions that are part of observable human experience.

Both qualitative data collection methods are used in this study, and the findings and conclusions in this report are based on both types of data.

Because the intention was to find the meaning of alcohol in everyday lives of poor people, a qualitative approach was regarded as the most fruitful method of data collection. The intention was to understand why people behave as they do, and to get people's own perception of their situation, of their attitudes and actions regarding alcohol use. Our intention was to get the actors' perspectives, their own definitions of the situation. This is expressed by William I. Thomas: "If men define situations as real, they are real in their consequences" (Cuff et al. 1992:152).

We also wanted to know something about their background, not only what they could tell us when we talked to them, but what it looked like to an outsider, a person who did not take for granted the things that the villagers themselves did or maybe had stopped noticing. Therefore the interviews were supplemented by observation. Our data collection methods are influenced by what Robin Room calls the ethnographic, "holocultural" approach to the analysis of drinking patterns (Room et al. 2002:80). He argues that this approach is useful in at least two ways:

- Even in preliterate societies, social control and social and political power relationships are important factors to consider in the study of drinking customs and the level of alcohol consumption.

- The drinking customs in every society are bound up with its overall cultural dynamics. These special features of culture and interaction probably have an autonomous impact on drinking patterns that cannot be explained by the material structure of the society.

We used different qualitative methods, and all of them will be presented and discussed here. The main approach however, was ten days each of observation and interviews, in nine different social settings:

- An over-crowded urban setting in Colombo, in a community that would commonly, and often slightly pejoratively, be named a 'slum'

- A dry zone village in Katharagama
- A dry zone village in Mihintale
- A dry zone village in Polonnaruwa
- A wet zone village in Avissawella
- A fishing village in Negombo
- A tea estate community in Kandy
- A village in Vavuniya with both native inhabitants and resettled internally displaced persons, (all Tamils and Hindus)
- A village of relocated, internally displaced Muslims in Puttalam

The settings were selected to cover different types of communities, from different parts of the country, people from different ethnic backgrounds and with different income sources. As the rural dry zone consists of very different economic features, we picked three different dry zone communities. In Polonnaruwa in the north we found a village where the economy was based on paddy cultivation. In Mihintale we found a poorer community, where the income came from chena cultivation and some paddy. The Katharagama village was situated close to the sacred town, where visiting pilgrims provide some income opportunities. This is combined with gem mining and chena cultivation. All these income sources are very unstable. The wet zone was represented by a village in Avissawella, in Ratnapura district. As the larger source of income was a rubber estate, this might not be representative of the wet zone.

The selection of villages within these different types of settings was done on basically a pragmatic basis. We followed the advice given in literature and selected settings where field work could be carried out with as few problems as possible (cf. Ryen 2002:80, Hammersley and Atkinson 1995). Even then, it turned out that several hardships had to be endured during the field work. As in most qualitative studies, many villages could be found that could fill our criteria for covering different types of social settings.

There were ten days field work in each village, with ten in-depth interviews, one each day. Decisions about the duration of field work are always difficult. In our study we wanted to stay long enough to get to know the village and the people, but because comparison was an intention, we had to give priority to visiting several villages instead of spending all the time at one place. The information that could be added by staying for example 20 days instead of 10, was probably relatively small (cf. Patton 1990:214)[4]

1.2.2 Field assistants for observation and interviews

Our research questions could have been addressed through a traditional anthropological approach. One way of doing this would have been to pick one village and to live there and stay there for a longer time, at least some months. However, "research, like diplomacy, is the art of the possible" (Patton 1990:13). In our study, it was impossible for the two researchers themselves to settle in the settings under study, for at least two reasons:

- It would have demanded resources far beyond what was available to us

Introduction and Methodology

- Even with greater resources it would still have been improbable that we could get completely valid information.

In our study the data collection was done by field assistants, trained for the purpose, and the data interpretation was done by the researchers. This could be a disadvantage, but it also adds some benefits. Literature on qualitative research usually underlines that the data for qualitative analysis typically come from fieldwork, where the researcher herself spends time in the setting under study. The researcher makes firsthand observations of activities and interactions, and talks to people about their experiences and perceptions. In traditional qualitative inquiries the researcher is the instrument (cf. Guba and Lincoln 1981:113).

The validity and reliability of qualitative data depend to a great extent on the methodological skill, sensitivity, and integrity of the researcher (Patton 1990:11). We had to depend on the skills and the sensitivity of our field assistants, based on what we experienced in the training sessions before they went to the field, and on the regular feedback sessions we had with them during their fieldwork.

In our study the field assistants were the instruments. So the guidelines for both the observation and the interviewing had to be far more explicit than usual. Actions and questions that would have been taken for granted by an experienced researcher in the field, had to be formulated and expressed. A common criticism of qualitative methods is that what is seen and heard by the researcher is filtered through his or her opinions and attitudes. We also took the opportunity to follow up and to probe regularly the findings of our field assistants. They had to explain for example why they found the living conditions miserable in a given community, and why they had asked certain questions from particular informants.

The field assistants were selected on basis of their communication skills, and trained by the researchers. The main requirement was that they should be able to communicate with people in the villages, and we chose not to use students in sociology or anthropology. The training involved role play, and also involved a focus on empathy, as that is an important aspect developing from personal contact with people interviewed and observed during fieldwork. Empathy involves being able to take and understand the stance, position, feelings, experiences and world view of others. Traditionally the role of the researcher is to have an open mind about what to look for. One of the major aspects in our training of field assistants, had to do with this open-mindedness. They should be open to whatever they experienced in the villages, and to whatever their informants wanted to tell them. Interviewers are not in the field to judge or change values and norms. They are there to understand the perspectives of others. Getting valid, reliable, meaningful information requires sensitivity to and respect for differences. On the other hand dialogue oriented interviews affect people. They lay open thoughts, feelings, knowledge and experience not only to the interviewer, but also to the informant. For some informants, our questions may have affected their attitudes and behaviour, particularly towards alcohol.

Studying alcohol and meanings related to alcohol use, poses many challenges. In many cultures, norms dictate the attitudes towards drinking, negative in some settings and situations, positive in others. People may in such a situation answer in a way that keeps them in line with the norms, rather than disclose their own experiences (cf. Skjelmerud 1999:40). They may want to tell the researcher what they assume the researcher wants to hear. It is often not easy to explain drinking, nor is it always easy to remember clearly what happened when drinking. In the interaction with our informants, our study was initially introduced as a research on the everyday life of poor people. The field assistants were trained to allow the informants themselves to put the question of alcohol use on the agenda. The interviews were open ended, and after a conversation about income sources and everyday life in the village, the assistants asked the informant to tell about the last wedding or funeral the informant had attended. This question almost always introduced the alcohol theme, and gave the field assistant the opportunity to follow up by other questions about the informant's experiences, both with his or her own alcohol consumption, and with the drinking habits of relatives and other villagers.

The field assistants were also trained to do active interviewing, to invite and assist narrative production and to regard the interview as a meaning-making process, with the informant as a storyteller (cf. Holstein and Gubrium 1995:29). The interviews were not so much dictated by a pre-designed set of specific questions, but loosely directed and constrained by the interviewer's topical agenda, objectives and queries.

All interviews, which lasted 1-2 hours, were taped, transcribed, and later translated into English. The tape recording was carried out with the informants' consent, and did not generally lead to any problems. The day-to-day follow up of the field assistants was done by three field co-ordinators.

1.2.3 Individual information about social activities

As drinking is a social activity, a group oriented approach might have been natural. The reason we chose to focus on individuals, was that a group approach is more complicated and more demanding for the person who is collecting the data, in our case the field assistant without any formal social science research background. To counteract the methodologically individualistic bias, where an isolated individual is being interviewed personally about his or her attitudes, behaviour and experiences, we deliberately asked the informants about their relationship to others, and we often collected information from people who knew each other well.

The individual interviews were supplemented by observation. The field assistants were to report what the place looked like, whether it looked clean and tidy, and to describe the water supply and the sanitary conditions. They also reported what the people looked like, whether they looked healthy, happy and content, and they were to observe people, including the children - whether the children looked healthy and clean, and how they were looked after. For information on our main theme, alcohol and drinking, the field assistants reported whether they could see people who appeared 'drunk', and at what time of day. They also observed and noted how other people reacted toward drunken behaviour - with acceptance, with a smile, or with open displeasure? And they observed the availability of alcohol, legal and illicit. The observation report turned out to be very useful, full of details not only about the issues mentioned above, but also about smells and flies, about friendliness and about the field assistants' feelings and personal experiences. Even if the researchers did not get the opportunity to visit the field sites themselves, these report gave a very vivid and good impression of the villages and the people living there.

However, although the field assistants lived in each community for ten days, our observation was not participatory in the strict meaning, unlike what happened in a previous study (Abeyasinghe 2002: 22 and 148). This restricted our information of drinking groups and drinking situations.

The selection of informants in a village always started by finding a key informant[5]. He or she had to be able to give information about the village and village life, and to introduce the assistant to nine other informants in the village. The assistants were instructed to look for someone such as the school teacher, the midwife or someone in a similar position, as key informant.

The other nine informants in each village were selected partly at random, to cover different age groups and both men and women. We also included an element of 'purposeful sampling', that is to select information-rich instances which could illuminate the questions under study (cf. Patton 1990:169)[6]. For example, if the opportunity was there, the assistant should try to get an interview with the kasippu seller in the village.

1.2.4 Some experiences from the field work

A murder in Katharagama

We describe here some experiences from the field assistants' stay in their villages. In the village in Kataragama, the field work in the setting was done by a young female field assistant, initially accompanied by a field co-ordinator. She had a hard time, first to convince her family that it was safe for her to go there on her own, and then during the field work. Neither her family nor we were able to predict that there was going to be a murder in the village during her stay there. On her fourth day, at around 10 in the night a man 'drunk on kasippu' had gone to a nearby village house. He had an argument with the woman there, hit her head with a pole and hacked her to death.

It seemed to the field assistant that this incident was just one of many for the villagers. One of the informants who were not greatly surprised, commented on the murder like this: *"It would have been strange if some deed like this had not been committed by him."* After the murder, people seemed to be afraid to give information to our researcher too. Some informants prepared one of their bedrooms for the field assistant to sit and talk so that they were not seen from the road. In spite of these problems, the field assistant went through with her interviews and spent her ten days in the village. The informants, five men and five women, all described the life in the village from their perspective.

The beauty of Mihintale compared to the polluted slum in Colombo

We also experienced that the succession of the different field work settings might produce a bias. One of our field assistants first spent ten days in a 'slum' community in Colombo, in a village literally situated on a garbage heap, a place with a foul odour, filled with flies and containing relatively unfriendly people. The same assistant went next to a village in Mihintale, a community that was very different. In one of the first sentences of the field report, he describes it as, *"a beautiful village covered with greenery and surrounded by a couple of dams"*. He goes on to say,

"a very quiet village completely different from the hassle of the towns I passed. The sounds and songs of the birds, which live in large numbers, magnify the beauty of the village. These sounds were heard during day and night. The breathtaking sight of the rock of Mihintalaya seen in the far distance is a gift for this village. The large "Nuga" trees have spread their roots and branches all over the area confirming their rights to this land. Not only these trees, but also the many "Mee", "Atamba" and "Asatu" trees all show the newcomer how ancient and proud this village is."

Apart from being a good description of the village, this might also be an indicator of the fact that the field assistant somehow fell in love with this village, and that this may have coloured his perception of what he experienced there.

It also seems that he was rather taken by the hospitality of the villagers:

"There was one thing common to all the houses I visited. As soon as you enter, the hosts would ask, in a very soft voice, whether you would like to drink a glass of water and immediately serve one. After that they would serve you food or tea. If you reject it, they will feel very upset and disappointed, but if you accept it they would be overjoyed."

Maybe our data from the village in Minhintale would have been slightly different if the field assistant had started his work here, and gone to the Colombo tenement later.

Harvesting season in Polonnaruwa

When the field work was restricted to ten days, the time of the year could also influence our findings. In the village in Polonnaruwa the data collection took place in what was a very busy time for the villagers. That could have influenced the field assistant's observations and the answers he got on his questions. The field assistant felt that the villagers were thinking a lot:

"It was as if they were always carrying some heavy weight in their heads. The rushing nature of the villagers disturbed the peacefulness and the calmness of the village. I think that this rush was because this was the Maha season and everybody was occupied in the paddy cultivation".

Christmas time in Negombo

Christmas was celebrated while our field assistant was in the fishing village in Negombo. Because this was a Christian village[7], the timing probably created bias in what he saw and heard[8]. He describes his experiences on Christmas day like this:

Introduction and Methodology

"On the 25th I felt that I was lost in a war field. The sound of the firecrackers and the cries of the crows with shouts and laughter of the children all blend together to show how the villagers were celebrating Christmas. The small children were running here and there. Among them were few who were wearing new clothes. The Church was getting ready for the singing of Carols. It was to start at 9 p.m.

The roads were covered with small pieces of paper. These were the leftovers of the hundreds of firecrackers lit. I hoped that someone would invite me for Christmas, but I was not so lucky. Drunken people were everywhere I looked. People were talking loudly and enjoying Christmas. Once in a while the sound of a fight was heard, but it disappeared with the sound of the firecrackers".

Hardship in the villages of internally displaced persons

The field assistant in our village of internally displaced persons in Puttalam had several problems, adding to the fact that he experienced the village as a rather depressing place to stay. Most of the methodological problems are actually indicators of the situation in each village. The difficulty in finding a key informant is maybe the best example. The field assistant found no one who stood out in the community in terms of education, employment, money or indeed authority. Even to find an 'Advanced Level' educated person was quite difficult. He noted that there are none in any stable government or private sector employment. Leaders change frequently and all that the current so-called leaders can do is to pitifully complain or despair.

Another indicator of the situation that complicated the interview situations was that any conversation with an outsider was quickly taken over with evident practice in showing and explaining their needs and requirements, by virtually one and all. *"Ah, so you are from an organisation; well we don't have this and this ……..; you could do this and this…………but if that is too difficult, you could try this and this……"* According to the field assistant they go on and on in what would be comical if not for the desperate nature of their requests. This invariably required an explanation from the outsider such as the field assistant explaining that we are just trying to understand the situation, and this may or may not lead to material help for this place.

It was also difficult to secure an interview alone with the informants. Even when an informant was isolated and sitting at the front of the house, he would keep turning every few minutes towards where the females were, for confirmation of what he was saying

In the village with internally displaced Tamil persons in Vavuniya, a different field assistant did the data collection. Due to practical problems (security, transport, facilities etc), he was not able to spend the nights in the village. He went through with his interviews, but his observations were limited to what he could see during daytime. That means that the data in this village is maybe less reliable than from other villages. For some reason the data also give little information on alcohol use.

1.2.5 Supplementary data from the urban setting

One part of this report focuses on the situation in the capital city, Colombo. The data for this section is gathered through the use of two methodologies. One source is similar to that of the study of areas outside Colombo – namely, the use of in-depth interviews with a key informant and nine others from the same community.

In the second methodology too, data was gathered through interviews with persons from selected communities or 'settings'. But in this component a setting was not a cluster of residences or homes. The residential community wasn't adequate to cover the different nuances of city life.

The 'informal entry'

What happens in a 'three-wheeler stand', a workplace or office, a bar cum restaurant or a shopping mall is as relevant to the subject under study, as what happens in a given residential commune. Some research assistants were consequently engaged to integrate with and study these non-residential *settings*. Since these are not 'residential', the location does not 'belong' to anybody, and the membership of the location is 'fluid'. In such instances there was less sense in, and possibility of, linking to a key person to introduce us to the setting. So a slightly different entry was used.

In these locations, initial discussions were with individuals engaged 'naturally'. The research assistant spent time in the place and gradually approached individuals there and engaged them in conversation. All the field assistants eventually selected for this component of the study were male. As little as possible of personal details of the research assistant were initially disclosed. Disclosure about what he 'did' was limited to the information that he had no permanent employment, which was true. Sometimes the field assistant said that he was currently working in collecting data for a research study.

The assistant had to spend as much time as required initially to integrate with the given setting and to develop links with key individuals there. At a restaurant, for example, the research assistant would visit as a customer a few times and make friends with some of the restaurant staff. In a few days he would be a known person in that setting and had opportunity to mix and talk to customers who came as individuals or as groups. He would sometimes be invited to sit with the group and participate in the conversation and the food and drink. He would have to pay for part of the expenses too.

Where a longer, or more focussed, interview with a particular person was felt likely to be useful the assistant indicated the nature of the research interest. Those selected were asked whether they would agree to provide more details. In the restaurant such a person could, for example, be someone serving customers there.

The persons selected as research assistants were those who succeeded in making links readily and easily with the selected settings. Potential field assistants were asked to make an initial 'trial' visit and provide feedback, after a brief introduction on how they should proceed. This allowed us to take on for training only those who showed capability in the real life activity.

Previous training in qualitative research methodology was not a selection criterion.

The advantage of this was that the assistants eventually selected were remarkably good at integrating with, and reflecting what prevailed within, the communities or settings selected. A disadvantage was that they did not have training in critical or objective analysis and reflection on 'superficial' reports or observations. This weakness was somewhat counteracted through regular and frequent discussions with and guidance from one of the researchers. The four individuals selected in this way had hardly any difficulty understanding and applying the ideas on critical analysis and follow up of informants' statements. A second disadvantage of this method was that it required rather a large investment of the researcher's time. This extra investment of time was felt to be justified because the innovation of using relatively less experienced (but more 'naturally' integrated) assistants required this. Thus they were debriefed by one of the researchers rather than a field coordinator.

In this method of data-gathering no tape recordings were used. The field assistant made detailed notes from memory immediately after the field visit. He later had to discuss his report and complete aspects of the notes that were incomplete or were found to be worthy of expansion. This was done before going out on the next day. In each of these sessions the field assistant would be brought back into line with the objectives of the study. They were told at each debriefing what material they brought had greater relevance to the study's objectives. Soon they learnt to focus increasingly on issues relevant to poverty and to alcohol.

The field assistants in this informal component were more intensively supervised than those in the other. One of the researchers (DS) had direct debriefings with each of them, initially every third day or so. He cross-questioned them on every aspect and then made suggestions to get them into line with the objectives of the study. The need to find out the existing reality rather than attempt to provide an image or idea of it that the field assistant believed would please the researchers was constantly emphasized. They were quite aware that a particular finding would not be more 'popular' with the researchers than another. All of the field assistants understood that only inaccurate findings were unacceptable.

1.2.6 Quantitative study

The major part of this study was on a qualitative investigation in several selected settings. We supplemented this with a small quantitative study conducted in each setting at the end of the in-depth qualitative component.

The quantitative study was not intended as a representative sampling of a particular universe. It was meant mostly to be a check on, and a broader sampling of, the same settings that were looked at in the qualitative phase.

Up to twenty informants were questioned from each setting where the qualitative study was conducted. The exact number questioned was based on a rough estimate of the relative size of the village or community sampled. In some settings a larger sample was taken to keep the total number of questionnaires roughly in proportion with ratios of particular population sub-groups. The data was gathered on an interviewer administered questionnaire (see appendix) asking about alcohol use, details of type, quantity and cost, alcohol-related behaviour and experiences, and perceptions of alcohol users as well as demographic details including income, debts and savings. The questionnaires were in Sinhala and Tamil and none were in English.

A total of 306 questionnaires were administered. The questionnaire was administered only on the last day of the field assistant's stay in a given setting. The interviewer was by then familiar to the community. The interviewer followed a prescribed schedule for selecting subjects. The proportion of male or female subjects selected from each setting was not allowed to be less than one third. Anonymity was assured. Names were not recorded.

1.2.7 Ethical considerations

Ethical standards followed are in compliance with the Norwegian Research Council's ethical guidelines for carrying out social science research (See *Norwegian Social Science Data Service*'s guidelines for Protection of Privacy: www.nsd.uib.no/english) Names of people have all been deliberately changed so that confidentiality can be maintained, and names of villages are concealed.

Photographs are intended to provide a flavour of the physical settings described. They have bee n taken from locations other than the actual setting described in the text. This has been done to maintain annonymity of individuals concerned. But the photographs have been selected from locations very similar to the actual study areas, so they do give an acurate image of the locality.

Notes

4. Patton's advice is both simple and pragmatic: "Fieldwork should last long enough to get the job done - to answer the research question being asked and to fulfil the purpose of the study."

5. A key informant is a person who is supposed to give information not only about him/herself, but also about the community that he or she is a part of. (Cf. Löfgren 1996).

6. Cf. Miles and Huberman who recommend the researcher to "go to the meatiest, most study-relevant sources" (1984:42).

7. There are both Tamils and Sinhalese living in the village, but all are Christians

8. Cf. Abeyasinghe (2002:61) who found that "the alcohol trade was doing a brisk business on Christmas day", in his study in the Colombo slum.

Results of quantitative study

2.1 Sample

Selected tables from the study are included below. We had 151 female and 155 male respondents.

The respondents were from 11 districts, with nearly a quarter (71) of them coming from the district of Colombo. The age, occupation and educational characteristics are given in the following table.

130 (43%) of our respondents told the interviewer that they had no employment. Probably most of these are housewives who don't count themselves as 'employed'.

26 respondents (9%) had never been to school, and 85 (28%) had less than 6 years of schooling. The extent to which this corresponds with the ability to read and write, we do not know. The literacy rate of Sri Lanka is estimated 90.2%[1].

Table 1 Respondents by age, occupation and education

		Percentage (n=306)
Age	15-25 yrs	23
	26-40 yrs	40
	41-55 yrs	27
	Above 56 yrs	10
Occupation	Daily paid job	29
	Small business	13
	Clerk or equivalent	09
	Not employed	43
	Self employed	07
Education	Never been to school	09
	Grade 1-5	28
	Grade 6-10	37
	Passed G.C.E.O'Level	27
Total		100

1. Source: http://www.cia.gov/cia/publications/factbook/geos/ce.html#People

Table 2 Financial characteristics of the sample

	Less than Rs. 500	Rs. 501-Rs. 1000	Rs. 1001-Rs. 2000	More than Rs. 2001	Total
Weekly income (n=306)	58.5 %	13.4%	16.3%	11.8%	100.0
Weekly expenditure (n=306)	63.7%	13.4%	14.1%	08.8%	100.0
Savings (n=306)	96.1%	01.6%	00.7%	01.6%	100.0
Amount in debt (n=306)	86.6%	01.6%	02.9%	08.8%	100.0

2.2 Alcohol use

Twenty percent (61 subjects) of those sampled consumed alcohol more than twice a week – less than half this number using it daily. Only 3 women used alcohol daily. Among 52 persons who used alcohol once a week or less there were 8 women. Sixty three percent (193 subjects – 140 women and 53 men) had never consumed alcohol.

The frequency of use, when examined in relation to level of education, showed that the highest proportion of daily drinkers was among those with least (formal) education. This proportion declined with increasing level of education.

Table 3 Frequency of alcohol use

	Percentage (n=306)
Daily	08
2-6 days per week	12
Once a week or even less	17
Never	63
Total	100

Drinking Location

When those who consume exclusively at 'a place where alcohol is sold illegally' are added to the numbers who do so at an illegal setting as well as a bar or at home the total is over 50 %.

Table 4 Drinking location

	Percentage (n=61)
A place where alcohol is sold illegally	41
At the bar	20
At home	16
Other	10
'Illegal' and bar	10
Illegal and home	02
Bar and home	02
Total	100

Table 5 Type of alcohol used

Type of Alcohol	Percentage (n=61)
Arrack	20
Beer	03
Kasippu	33
Other	03
Arrack and beer	10
Arrack and kasippu	18
Arrack and other	02
Arrack, beer and kasippu	08
Arrack, beer and other	03
Total	100

Type of Alcohol Used

Of the 61 frequent (twice a week or more) users only two reported drinking beer. In the further breakdown into daily versus 2-6 days a week users, 60% of daily users use kasippu exclusively and another 20% use kasippu as well as some other alcoholic drink. For other frequent drinkers, the percentages using kasippu are 14% and 28%. Removing the kasippu outlets should make a big difference to the daily drinkers and their wives and children.

2.3 Money spent on alcohol

Expenditures on alcohol, we found in our qualitative study, are underreported for several reasons. This is not only due to people wanting to hide their true consumption. The reported expenditures in the questionnaire study showed that 19 subjects spent more than Rs. 100 per day on alcohol, 9 of whom reported an income of less than Rs. 500 per week. Thus the reported expenditure on alcohol among almost half the number of daily drinkers exceeds their reported income. This 'inconsistency' may simply be due to deliberate or unwitting misreporting. But there is, in addition, much greater 'unnoticed' alcohol expenditure due to a variety of other reasons that we elicited in the qualitative study – which is described later.

A little over 7% of men said that their alcohol expenditure was greater than their income. This is a small percentage but still a frightening statistic for the families concerned and for those interested in helping the worst-off families uplift themselves. A similar number of men will probably be spending close to or nearly all of their income on alcohol alone. Together this constitutes over 10% of our sample. The proportion of this severely compromised population is likely to be higher than 10%, when we take into account the identified underreporting of

Table 6 Expenditure on alcohol

	Amount	Percentage (n=61)
Daily	Less than Rs 50	44
	Rs 51 -Rs 100	25
	More than Rs 101	31
Monthly	Less than Rs 500	53
	Rs 501 - Rs 1000	13
	Rs 1001 - Rs 2000	21
	More than Rs 2001	13
Total		100

alcohol expenditure. These expenses are probably in the abjectly poor or poorest families. So any 'development' efforts that want to help the worst off cannot leave the alcohol issue untouched. If they do, they run the risk of helping those who are 'easier' to help whilst probably leaving out of their purview the most deprived and alcohol-compromised families. And we found that these constitute quite a significant number.

2.4 Behaviour after alcohol use

We asked about the perception that alcohol leads to boisterousness and fights. Almost 80% of respondents reported that when people are 'drunk' they have more fights and clashes than at other times. This perception was reported mostly by those who never consumed alcohol (89%), while 64% of daily drinkers and 36% of those who drank 2-6 days per week said the same – referring to their own behaviour when drunk.

When only 64% of daily drinkers claim that they become aggressive and while boisterous and 89% of abstainers say that people become aggressive the discrepancy can be put down to the daily drinkers not being sensitive to or deliberately not reporting their own aggressiveness after alcohol. Only a minority (36%) of those who drank 2 to 6 days a week say that they become more aggressive when drunk. This could be due to the fact that more of the 'alcohol-related' aggression and violence is committed by (the far fewer) daily drinkers. Or those who drank 2 – 6 days a week were even more keen than the daily users (perhaps identified 'problem drinkers') to conceal any problems on their part.

A less threatening question was whether people became more noisy or less so when they were drunk. This was asked before the question of aggressive behaviour. A slightly larger proportion of respondents (82%) said yes. Once again, it was the abstainers who mostly said so (90%). Again there were fewer (68%) of daily drinkers and fewest (42%) of people drinking 2 – 6 days saying this. Since 'making more noise' has no great connotation of 'misbehaviour' the lower report of noisiness too by the 2 – 6 days-a-week drinkers is probably more valid. We can assume that they are probably less in the habit of becoming noisier or becoming aggressive after alcohol use.

Table 7 Drunken behaviour-fighting

Behaviour	Daily or frequent drinkers[1] Percentage (n=61)	Abstainers or infrequent drinkers[2] Percentage (n=245)
More fights	48	87
Less fights	21	05
No difference	31	08
Total	100	100

Table 8 Drunken behaviour-noisiness

Behaviour	Daily or frequent drinkers[1] Percentage (n=61)	Abstainers or infrequent drinkers[2] Percentage (n=245)
Less noise	21	07
More noise	53	89
No difference	26	04
Total	100	100

1 When you are "drunk" how do you behave?
2 When people are "drunk" how do they behave?

1 When you are "drunk" how do you behave?
2 When people are "drunk" how do they behave?

Results of Quantitative Study

This difference is relevant to understanding the 'causes' of alcohol-induced disinhibition and aggressiveness. In this sample we found the phenomenon commoner in the daily drinkers than the 2 – 6 days-a-week drinkers. This may be because the daily drinkers have been drinking longer. It may take longer to graduate to the state of becoming 'disinhibited' after alcohol. Daily drinkers have probably been drinking for longer and so have had more time to 'learn' this behaviour. Or it may be because the daily drinkers were older (more than 65% over 25 years of age versus 42% over 25 years among the others) and therefore had anyway more authority to be loud or aggressive.

2.5 Subjective effect of alcohol

Our questionnaire did not try to separate the 'chemical' from other effects of alcohol, but asked people how they felt after alcohol use or what they believed people experienced after drinking alcohol. About half (157 or 51%) said they or others felt more happy after alcohol while 39% (120) gave 'less happy' as the experience. Less than 10% said there was no effect. 'More happy' as the feeling experienced after drinking alcohol was more commonly given by more frequent users (66%) while lower proportions of occasional users (58%) and abstainers (45%) said so.

Over 16% of daily users reported that they felt less happy after drinking alcohol. Nearly half of never-users believed that people felt less happy after drinking alcohol. Whether the latter were referring to people feeling 'unhappy' that they had consumed alcohol rather than finding the experience itself unpleasant is not clear.

Table 9 Subjective effect of alcohol- more or less happy

Behaviour	Daily or frequent drinkers[1] Percentage (n=61)	Abstainers or infrequent drinkers[2] Percentage (n=245)
Less happy	12	46
More happy	66	48
No difference	23	06
Total	100	100

[1] After you drink alcohol how do you feel?
[2] What does a person feel after drinking alcohol?

A large number (237 or 77%) said that alcohol led to more crying and talking about problems than the non-alcohol state. Over 80% of occasional and never users said people cry more after alcohol use while only 56% of daily drinkers and 47% of 2 –6 days a week drinkers said so. Once again, the 2 – 6 days-a-week drinkers do not fall in-between the daily drinkers and the occasional or non-users.

Table 10 Subjective effect of alcohol- crying or grumbling

Behaviour	Daily or frequent drinkers[1] Percentage (n=61)	Abstainers or infrequent drinkers[2] Percentage (n=245)
Cry or talk about problems less	13	07
Cry or talk of problems more	51	84
No difference	36	09
Total	100	100

[1] After you drink alcohol how do you feel?
[2] What does a person feel after drinking alcohol?

Finally, we asked directly about the pleasantness or unpleasantness of the act of drinking alcohol as well as that of 'being drunk'. The act of drinking was rated as a pleasant and easy experience by 98 subjects (32%) while 'being drunk' was reported as pleasant and easy by just 42 (14%). The change from pleasant to unpleasant between the 'act of drinking' and 'being drunk' was found among all levels of consumption, but the least change was among daily drinkers. Fourteen daily drinkers of 25 (56%) had reported the act of drinking as pleasant and easy while 12 reported that being drunk too was so. In all other levels of consumption, there was a much larger proportion that changed their assessment. Of those who consumed alcohol once a week or less as many as 63% (33 of 52) said that the act of drinking was an unpleasant or uncomfortable experience while 41 of them (79%) reported that being drunk was unpleasant or uncomfortable.

2.6 Image of alcohol users

Fifty nine percent of respondents rated alcohol users as less attractive than others and 20 % found them more attractive – with a similar number seeing no difference. Perhaps unsurprisingly, among those who reported drinking twice a week or more (including daily) a smaller proportion (34%) thought alcohol users were less attractive than others and 33% thought that they were more attractive. Sixty five percent of abstainers and occasional users thought users were less attractive.

Alcohol users were rated stronger than the others by 97 and weaker or inferior to others by 150 (49%). Among frequent users 57% thought they were stronger and 23% that they were weaker. The proportions being in the opposite direction among the abstainers and occasional users. On enjoyment of life, the majority rated alcohol users lower than the others 62% versus 23%. The opinion of 48% of frequent drinkers was that users enjoyed life more while 34% still felt that they enjoyed life less than non-users.

Table 11 Evaluation of the act of drinking alcohol

Behaviour	Daily or frequent drinkers[1] Percentage (n=61)	Abstainers or infrequent drinkers[2] Percentage (n=245)
Is pleasant and easy	59	25
Is unpleasant and difficult	23	65
Neither pleasant or unpleasant	18	10
Total	100	100

1 When you are drinking alcohol how do you feel?
2 What does a person feel, when drinking alcohol?

Table 12 Evaluation of being "drunk"

Behaviour	Daily or frequent drinkers[1] Percentage (n=61)	Abstainers or infrequent drinkers[2] Percentage (n=245)
Is pleasant and easy	31	09
Is unpleasant and difficult	43	83
Neither pleasant or unpleasant	26	07
Total	100	100

1 When 'drunk' how do you feel?
2 What does a person feel when 'drunk'?

Results of Quantitative Study

Table 13 Image of alcohol user-attractiveness

Image	Daily or frequent drinkers[1] Percentage (n=61)	Abstainers or infrequent drinkers[2] Percentage (n=245)
Less attractive	34	65
More attractive	33	18
No difference	33	18
Total	100	100

Table 14 Image of alcohol user-strength

Image	Daily or frequent drinkers[1] Percentage (n=61)	Abstainers or infrequent drinkers[2] Percentage (n=245)
Stronger than others	57	25
Less strong (more submissive) than others	23	56
No difference	20	19
Total	100	100

The majority of frequent users (29 vs. 21) felt that alcohol users enjoy life more rather than less, compared to non-users. This is in keeping with the common perception that alcohol use is 'fun'. The relatively small majority is rather surprising, especially since this is among a group regularly and frequently using alcohol.

Abstainers and occasional users on the other hand felt overwhelmingly (170 vs. 42) that alcohol users in fact enjoyed life less than non-users. This is quite contrary to the perception that alcohol use promotes fun and enjoyment and that abstainers are killjoys.

On one characteristic alone, a clear majority of even the daily or frequent gave a 'negative' opinion about alcohol users. This was on whether alcohol users were less intelligent or more intelligent than the others.

The combined totals for all 306 of the sample showed that 151 (49%) thought users were less intelligent while 21 (7%) said they were more so. This was the characteristic with the starkest reported difference. Even among the 61 daily or frequent users, a clear majority (23 against 11) thought that alcohol users, namely they themselves, were less intelligent than 'non-users'.

Table 15 Image of alcohol user-enjoying life

Image	Daily or frequent drinkers[1] Percentage (n=61)	Abstainers or infrequent drinkers[2] Percentage (n=245)
Enjoys life more	48	17
Enjoys life less	34	69
No difference	18	14
Total	100	100

Table 16 Image of alcohol user-intelligence

Image	Daily or frequent drinkers[1] Percentage (n=61)	Abstainers or infrequent drinkers[2] Percentage (n=245)
Less intelligent	38	52
More intelligent	18	9
No difference	44	39
Total	100	100

2.7 Comment

Each of these findings calls for much discussion and speculation, especially regarding possible causality among these associations. Even more discussion is possible about the direction of any possible causality. Are alcohol users less intelligent and less attractive than others, as the majority of our respondents seem to think? If indeed they are, does the alcohol use cause or result from the characteristic?

More significant perhaps is that the proportions who gave opinions about any of the characteristics concerned were very similar between daily users and those who used alcohol 2–6 days a week. And their opinions diverged widely from the others. The 'others' were the occasional alcohol users (once a week or less) and the abstainers. Abstainers and occasional users appear very close to each other in all their evaluations.

In fact, the occasional drinkers and abstainers had close to identical proportions holding the same opinion on nearly all of the preceding parameters. So we combined the results of abstainers and occasional users into one column. The opinions of daily and frequent users (2 to 6 days a week) too were combined for the same reason.

The terms 'alcohol user' and 'abstainer' are frequently and readily used in Sri Lanka. This terminology creates a division along an artificial line, it appears. The more 'natural' line appears to be between the occasional user and non-user population on the one hand and the frequent (daily and twice week or more) users on the other.

The rural poor live on earnings from their family members who work in Colombo. The rural rich make their money mostly by selling to Colombo or bringing back money earned in Colombo. There is no significant urban centre other than Colombo. Kandy and Jaffna are the only cities that have potential to develop any degree of autonomous existence in the near future.

Colombo gets from all of the rest of the country, among other things, a workforce. And the city in return provides them not only with money, but also with normative ideas, attitudes and fashions.

A significant proportion of the rural rich, middle class and poor spend a significant time living or working in the city. The movement between city and village is continuous and massive. Many travel daily long distances from rural home to city workplace. Large numbers travel home at weekends from city 'boardings' (hostels) where they reside to work or study. So much that is new is learnt in the city and instantly transferred to the village. Equally large numbers travel 'home' monthly or every two to three months. This is because they live in more distant villages or don't have breaks or leave on a weekly basis. They take home a larger amount of money along with their city training.

Patterns of expenditure and aspirations for life for the rural person are therefore strongly influenced by the same factors that influence the city dweller. Residence in a village is for many just a matter of having a home outside the city. Much of life is probably spent in the city by a fair number of those classified as rural dwellers.

COLOMBO

Colombo is where everything comes together

Colombo

An overcrowded residential setting I

Our sources

The impressions from Colombo are derived from the reports of a few research assistants who sampled a cross section of city life, using both methodologies described in Chapter 2. One source is similar to that of the study on areas outside Colombo, where the field assistant obtained the broader picture through a key informant in an interview lasting several hours and then through nine other informants – also interviewed at depth. The interviews were tape-recorded and transferred into a hand-written text document on the same day. The community studied through this methodology was an urban under-serviced area (called by some a 'slum'), described first.

The rest of the data was gathered using a somewhat different methodology. This methodology applied to all the settings other than the first setting described immediately following this paragraph. In the other settings we did not focus on a 'geographically defined' residential cluster of homes. That method alone, we realized, wasn't adequate to get a complete feel of events and currents in Colombo. The second approach, described in the preceding chapter (on methodology) as the 'informal entry', was used therefore to supplement the first.

This village fits into what is commonly called an 'urban slum community', but this particular overcrowded setting is different from others. In this location, the whole of the community and life is dominated by a huge garbage dump. The village sits on the border of the dump. This alone makes this rather atypical amongst settings referred to as 'slum communities'.

Our field assistant and coordinator report that one of their most striking experiences was the overpowering smell that hit them as they approached the village. It was unlike anything they had experienced before.

The smell came from the living, expanding and horribly ugly dump. The garbage collection is over 15 metres in height and about 1 km in length. Lorries bring garbage to the dump and bulldozers pile it up. People work on the dump, constantly flattening and spreading out the garbage heap. The smell is overpowering to a newcomer, as it was so to our field assistant. The local residents seem to have accepted it, or adjusted to it.

There is also a stagnant 'lake' along the railway line, which forms another 'border' for the village. This too is polluted and smelly and probably a good breeding ground for mosquitoes. The whole village seemed to be a breeding place for flies. There were many unhealthy looking stray dogs and many crows, but the flies dominate all. Flies are everywhere in large numbers.

It seems that there are no off peak hours for traffic in Colombo. Traffic jams, overflowing pavements and pollution all contribute to the milieu.

As one crosses the railway line and enters the village there is a boutique. It sells many food items and other provisions. Right next to it are a few storerooms, which store waste materials. Opposite those storerooms is a three-wheeler stand, and the drivers of these vehicles can constantly be seen standing around. They did not look very pleasant. They seemed to be 'tough guys' too, but the research assistant wondered whether this was put on, as a show.

Our field assistant saw a few young men smoking ganja (cannabis) in the shade of a tree by this lake. This was at around 10 o'clock in the morning.

3.3.1 Environment and facilities

There is a community centre in the village, and the preschool is held in this community centre. The surroundings of the preschool too were very dirty.

There are two public wells and a toilet. Most of the villagers use the public toilet. There are few public taps, and villagers use it for all purposes. Washed dishes and pots could be seen near those taps at any time of the day. The water does not get drained properly. Therefore stagnant polluted water could be seen collected near the taps. And more flies.

Most of the houses are made of wood, and there were usually two rooms in each house. One room is used for cooking. The houses are adjacent to each other, with no gaps in between. Only three houses were built in brick, bigger and better than the rest. These houses are walled or separated from their neighbour's.

Footpaths between the rows of houses were not clean. The rail track was also polluted with dumped garbage and littered with empty cigarette packs.

Few houses have electricity, and the rest use oil lamps. There are a few houses, which are kept clean compared to others. The bigger houses even had carpeted floors. The members of those families looked healthier and cleaner than other families. In some houses the garden is kept clean. Most houses have televisions and radios. Car batteries power these. They frequently watch Tamil movies and TV channels like "Sirasa" and "Swarnavahini". Walls of most houses were covered with pictures of film actors. Most of them are Indian actors.

There are about four houses that collect and sell 'waste' metals to the market.

There is a small 'devala' or shrine to a God, which is a small room built in wood. There were few boutiques in the village. These boutiques sell kasippu (illicit spirits) too. They also sell prepared snacks ('vadey'), and there were many people in each of those boutiques.

Several societies and organizations function in the village. A 'funeral assistance society' ('Maranadara Samithiya'), Community Development Society ('Prajasanwardana Samithi'), and 'FORUT' are examples.

3.3.2 The people and their life style

The village has about 170 families, Sinhalese, Muslims and Tamils. Our field assistant couldn't say confidently which

In a country where the majority depend on public transport, overcrowded buses and trains bring in hundreds of thousands into Colombo daily from the rest of the country. The city provides them not only with money, but also with normative ideas, attitudes and fashions.

group was larger, but the Muslims appeared somewhat fewer. There were people who had been living in this village for 50-60 years. There were also people who had settled in that area recently.

General mood

Our field assistant's overall general comment about the people is that they are mostly frustrated and angry. It is unlike the description of any other community. The general mood is described as one of unfriendliness, almost hostility.

The majority in this village were felt to be living their lives in fear and suspicion. The village was believed to be one that provided protection to certain powerful characters. They were said to control the village (eg. taking decisions concerning the people of the village). Some residents felt that these powerful persons may feel threatened if the people of the village become more educated or if the village develops further. They would see it as a threat to their activities or control.

Many see the powerful characters in a positive light. They are seen as 'heroes' who help them in their need. They have created an environment where no one can go against them, but, there are people who are 'waiting for their chance' to do so. At the same time, many youths in the village treat them as role models and try to follow their lead. The children in the village follow the youth.

Whether our informants spoke only of positive attributes of the powerful characters due to their genuine impression being positive is difficult to determine. People may not have trusted our researchers enough to be confident of saying negative things about them. The equivalent of the word 'thugs' (*'chandiyo'*) was sometimes used to describe the people who wielded power.

"Say an underworld character passes by when we are playing, someone would say something nice about his body or his attitude etc. Being a thug is very helpful. You can always get what you want. Our guys too want to be thugs. But there is an element of suspicion and fear."

Another feature of the general mood was that of low expectations. It was almost as if they don't care about their lives, according to our field assistant. Their lives have become hopeless. Interpersonal relationships too are at a low level. They wait for someone to come and help them. They think that you need to be wealthy to be happy in life, but not many have become wealthy. And not many think that they will ever become wealthy.

Insecurity

Apart from the unfriendliness another striking feature was that of expressed insecurity about the permanence of their living here. People say they are not sure how long they will be allowed to live here, and this is given as a reason for not improving their houses or living conditions.

"Only the first few houses are built in brick. We were told by the Oil Corporation that we would not be paid any compensation if we build our houses in brick. Most of the villagers want to leave this area. Most have bought land from outside."

The smell came from the living, expanding and horribly ugly dump. Lorries bring garbage to the dump and bulldozers pile it up. People work on the dump, constantly flattening and spreading out the garbage heap. The smell is overpowering to a newcomer. Local residents seem to have accepted it, or adjusted to it.

The field assistant felt that their expectations were not very high. There was said to be little thought of tomorrow. Their households and they themselves, the field assistant found, are not very clean. They don't think of their homes as their own. They live in a world of uncertainty, almost as if they expect their homes to be broken down tomorrow. They believe that someone will give them a new house in place of their current one. This is probably the only way to survive the insecurity, as nobody has the necessary funds to build a house on their own, and no family has even a plan to build a house of their own.

"This house is not our own. We don't have homes. These were given to us for temporary residence. If these are broken, we have no place to go. That is what we are thinking about right now."

It is not very clear whether they really believe that they can be just evicted by the authorities. Or they may be saying that they are insecure. This may allow them to continue in the current way of life with no attempt to 'improve themselves' – especially with regard to getting a house of their own to live in. Whether the feeling of insecurity is a way of protecting themselves from having to make unrewarding efforts to progress is difficult to surmise.

3.3.3 Freedom

Powerful and big businessmen in and around the village provide jobs and help at times of need. In return, the village provides them with people to work in their different tasks at a relatively low cost. This was seen by some as taking advantage of the village and the villagers.

Some felt that having a community that is very submissive suits the purpose of these powerful individuals. These people do help people in times of difficulty too. Our field assistant felt that this too may have contributed to making the villagers lethargic and rather low in their expectations. Some villagers believed that there is a relationship between the underworld gang members and the big businessmen. They feel that the underworld gang members run the village according to the needs of these businessmen.

"One businessman helps the villagers a lot. He gives out about one thousand rupees a month for the poor. Before he came, this place was not like as it is right now. The houses were different. He came and started managing the garbage dump and built new temporary houses along the rail track. Although they say it is temporary, we have lived here about five years. Once the underworld gang leader came to this village he asked the businessman to build better houses. And he immediately responded and built better houses in a better part of the village, in place of the temporary houses. It happened because of the boy ('Lamaya' or underworld gang leader)".

There are said to be underworld gang members, and their brokers, who do most of the illegal work in the village. They are said to control the sale of illicit alcohol ('kasippu') and illegal drugs. They also get other people in the village involved in their work by providing jobs for the unemployed. The youths who leave school are the primary recipients. Other people join the 'underworld' groups, just to 'build their image'. Some school-children try to

Most of the houses are made of wood, and there were usually two rooms in each house. One room is used for cooking. The houses are adjacent to each other, with no gaps in between.

follow their lead. It was suggested that the enthusiasm among youths to get involved with this type of work may come from their movie idols too.

"I take the lead in all activities of our village. Nobody can do anything without my knowledge. I get to know those things if someone hides them. Then I go and look for it and decide whether it is a good or a bad thing. If it is a bad thing, I make sure that they do not do it.

"There is a guy in this village who was involved in underworld acts. He is not in the village these days. He is a leader in our village. All villagers respect him, and he also loves the village. He helps the villages very often. Ten months back, he donated white clothes to all the children in our village. There are a few men who work for him. They also contact me before they do something."

Privacy
People appear to move in and out of others' houses with little regard for privacy. But it did appear that the few rich people (two or three families) in the village were a little more isolated from the rest of the community. So people in the community didn't all walk into the slightly wealthier house as freely as they do the other, less affluent, houses. There was at least a fence surrounding the wealthier person's property, and they had a gate that could be shut. Others could walk into anybody's house and talk to the householders freely. There were no walls or fences with gates separating the houses.

Racism
Although people are not particularly friendly towards each other, there is hardly any 'racial' antagonisms.

'There are no problems among different ethnic groups in our village'.

Pace of life
People move at a strange pace. Even after 9 o'clock in the morning many young men and women were seen still brushing their teeth and talking to others. Children aged 6-7 years were seen defecating along the railway track at this time. The children looked dirty. Most children carried sticks in their hands and they were crying or shouting most of time. Some children had wounds all over the body. Some were scratching their bodies all the time. Children 4–5 years old often used words like 'maranawa' (I'll kill you). They seemed to be neglected too. No adults were around to look after them. Young adults were also seen among them, and they used obscene language towards the children. Even the adults passing by addressed them in unfriendly or nasty names. ('ado', 'bada').

Children, men and women
Some mothers seemed to be angry with their children. This was evident even by the way they carried their children and the way they spoke to them. Children and adults looked wasted.

The men in the village, our field assistant concluded, have largely abandoned their responsibilities. It seemed to him that they were 'lifeless'. The women were more active.

Most of the structures were make-shift such as the house in the top photograph. There were a few houses built in bricks, bigger and better than the rest.

Most of the men in the village carry cigarettes or rolls of ganja (cannabis). There is a small house in the midst of the village, and there were men who were drinking kassippu. They were shouting loudly, drunk even at 11 am. Other villagers showed no concern about it.

Most of the villagers looked very rough, and the women also looked very domineering. Many youngsters gather along the railway line, and most of them have a cigarette in their hands. Some of them are smartly dressed. There are a few other young men who look wasted. Some of them were carrying metal pieces or poles in their hands. Some young men leave early in the morning, for work. They are to be seen in the afternoon. Several were said to work in the fish market. When they go out of the village, they dress nicely and fashionably.

The women were more active in the village, but most of them, our field assistant felt, were tired and exhausted. They get married at a very young age and have troubled marriages. The basic needs of the children of the village are not well met. As a consequence the level of nutrition, health and education is at a very low level.

"I have four children. Two are in a children's home. The other two are at home. One is a eleven-year-old girl and the other is a boy. It is very difficult to find someone who has schooled up to grade 8 in this village."

Women in the village are more active and they are involved in maintaining social relationships. Some women are fashionable. Most women hang around the public tap and the well. They observe what is happening in the surroundings. Women too make obscene jokes and use bad language. Most women do their cooking at the main door of their house, so they can observe what is happening in the surrounding. Once their work is over, they sit at their doorstep and chat with their neighbours. It is the women who are mostly involved in various societies in the village.

There are unmarried women who have two or three children. Husbands are generally suspicious about their wives, and if the wife is late in getting home after work, the husband suspects that the wife is selling sex. 'Everything ends up in a fight'. There are about 2 or 3 families in the village where the women are known to be 'prostitutes'.

The woman who sells kassippu was very talkative, and she frequently argued with her clients. There were also mothers carrying their children among them.

Education

Some adults were not educated, meaning that they had little formal schooling. Most children quit school when they reach grade 6-7. Some start working in garages while some join tea shops or stores.

"There are children who have studied up to O/L. Most of them are not employed because the salary is not adequate. Some are not motivated to look for a job. They just stay at home. There is a sister who helps the villagers to find jobs. I have helped most young men to find jobs, but they are not keen."

Colombo

Leisure

A good part of leisure time is spent on watching television, mainly 'Swarnavahini' and 'Sun TV'. These channels show Tamil films, and most of these are telecast during the morning or afternoon. There are television sets in most houses, and those who do not have one, go to a friend's house to watch movies. Many of the residents speak both Sinhala and Tamil.

"Since many people gather, we are not bored. Time flies. We just have fun. This is our life."

"During leisure we get together and play cricket, either in the ground or the road alongside the rail track."

Several young men can be seen reading the results of previous days horse races. They are usually disappointed with their defeats.

Hostility and solidarity

People quarrel with each other even for small misunderstandings. Sometimes those arguments go on for a long time. These problems are usually among women. The husbands usually do not get involved in such disputes.

Despite the lack of cooperation and the quarrelling, there are things on which people do get together. If there is a death in the village, all villagers get together and help with the funeral. This may cost about Rs. 7000. Similarly, parents contribute to run the Montessori school. The sister at the church started a Montessori for the kids, employing two teachers. Now they have to be paid with what ever is collected from the children. In the past she used to help financially, but now she doesn't do so as much.

"It's the fault of the people. They started making up various stories. It's not like those days. People are different. This is why the sister stopped helping."

Envy

Our field assistant did report that all in all the social relationship between the people of the village is neither pleasant nor refreshing. This he attributes to envy of one another and jealousy and suspiciousness of others.

"The people said, thanks to Priyanthi that child found a children's home and that the child is happy to be there. Probably this made that woman feel a bit inferior. She said that it wasn't Priyanthi who did it; it was I who found the home for the child. When I went to question this we got into a quarrel."

3.3.4 The economy

There are several people who work in the Colombo Municipal Council. Some work on a temporary basis, and in about ten families there are people with permanent jobs. Some are masons, and some work in tea stores. There are carpenters and people involved in different businesses (selling vegetables etc.). Some are daily earners, some get their salary monthly and people who work in private "Cleaning services" get their salary weekly.

People spend their money on different things. Some deposit it in "FORUT" related credit schemes. Some spend their money daily without saving it. Some people give the money to a 'seettu'. This is a system of people getting together to contribute a sum of money every month. One person collects money from all the members of the seettu, and the collection goes to each contributor in turn.

"There is no permanent job for most people in this village to lead a good family life. Therefore life is difficult. There isn't enough income even to repair or improve our homes. This house is not mine. It belongs to my wife's parents. They have two houses, the one in which they live and this one. My father-in-law works in a company and the mother-in-law works at Kotahena. They understand our difficulties and they help us.

"I have joined a seettu. I collect fifty rupees a day to pool for it. It's five hundred rupees a month. I recently found some work and earned five hundred rupees. I have already spent one hundred. We buy things on credit. If I'm unable to, my father-in-law pays.

In case of an emergency we borrow money from some one. This is a loan, but we don't have to pay interest for it if it is from a friend. We don't borrow from moneylenders. If we do we will fall into trouble."

When people are unable to pay back their loans, they have to mortgage their jewellery to pay their debts. There are pawnbrokers in the village itself, but the villagers are reluctant to go to them because they expect a large return.

There is a powerful businessman behind the scenes. He donates about ten thousand rupees when there is a funeral. He gives thousand rupees a month for any elderly person in the village.

'He helps the villagers, but at the same time he earns from them'.

"There used to be big houses with large land areas. He built small houses in that land. That way he earned a lot. He is the one who helps the villagers in any need."

A lot of money is said to drain out of the village through the use of drugs. Heroin users spend all they earn to buy drugs. The dealers in turn spend their money on arrack, cigarettes, to pay off the police, and for court cases. People spend much money gambling. This has become a fashion and is catching on among some of the youth in the village too.

"There is another lot who gamble with cards. Everyday they play cards before coming home and lose all their money. If there is no-one playing, they get hold of two to play and initiate on their own. They lose all the money they earn. There

The income of many workers was clearly higher than that of the staff in the shop, but they seem somehow to be unable to escape poverty.

is no food for the wife and the children. They also bet on horse racing. It's mostly the elderly who are addicted to this. Usually the young people are not into this, but most of them don't have jobs either. God knows how they find money to bet."

Our field assistant reports, 'It is difficult for me to understand the way money enters this village. The majority of people do not have permanent jobs. I feel that there is a hidden way of earning apart from the normal way we see from outside, but the money that this village earns, does not stay here for long'.

"Most of those who earn are daily paid workers. Some of them work in tea stores. Some work as helpers at various building sites. Some people do various kinds of small-scale business. Some women work as labourers at a cleaning agency and some others work as domestic helps."

Our field assistant continues to speculate, 'There must be ways in which more money flows into the village. But due to the lack of proper management, the funds do not stay in the village. They drain at the rate of entry or even faster'.

The moneylenders and pawnbrokers probably take quite a bit of money from the people in times of need. These are the few rich men in the village. They live in the well-built houses and lead middle class lives.

3.3.5 Alcohol and other substance use

There are several places in the village, which sell illicit arrack and ganja.

The majority of those who drink daily say that they do so because it helps them to get rid of the exhaustion after a hard day's work. They normally do not drink alone. One person buys a quarter bottle and another may buy half a bottle, and they all drink together. Those who consume alcohol regularly are said to be those with various 'problems'. The common perception is that these people are often reminded of their problems, even at work, and this drives them towards alcohol.

There are many people who use illicit drugs too on a daily basis. The informants claimed that heroin users spend about Rs. 1000 per day. This is not to say that the illicit drug users on average earn over Rs 1,000 a day for drugs. They get their money for drugs from their parents or spouses who earn money with great difficulty. Earlier they robbed other houses, but the villagers has taken actions against this, so now they do not do it anymore. People are not so ready to say that these daily drug users are using these substances because of 'problems'. This may be stated by those who consume the drugs, but others do not offer this as an explanation, which they do in the case of the regular alcohol users.

Nobody could guess the amount of money spent on alcohol, in relation to that spent on heroin.

Althogh men are traditionally regarded as breadwinners many families depend on the income earned by women. This was especially so in families where the males regularly use alcohol or other drugs.

Daily use of heroin is seen to serve a different function, or to be due to a different reason, from daily use of alcohol. And celebratory use of alcohol serves a different function from daily use.

Alcohol is, for example, an essential item for a wedding. In fact some people judge the quality of the wedding by the alcohol served. If alcohol is not served, it is a poor quality event. Alcohol is served at all functions of this village. People create trouble if alcohol is not served. Usually people have their weddings in reception halls because their houses are too small. People drink and dance and enjoy the event. If alcohol is not served in a wedding, they will bring it from outside. There are no parties without alcohol. If arrack is not served, they regard that family as very poor.

"The villagers usually have their weddings at a reception hall. It costs around five hundred rupees to book a hall. We go the previous night to help. The guys usually have a drink when they go for it. At the wedding itself alcohol is served at a separate table. Sometimes it is served at the dining table as well. There are no Kasippu dealers around here, but there are a few further down the road."

"From what I earned working abroad, I built a house for my mother and celebrated the weddings of my brother and sister. I have spent all what I have earned."

"I celebrated the wedding very simply. Since there wasn't enough room in the house we had to book a hall. I had to pay for alcohol, cigarettes, the cook etc. This is how all the money went"

3.3.6 Symbolism of alcohol

The people in the village seem to look at the use of alcohol as sign of prestige. They also see it as a part of life. The number of bottles served in a party or any other occasion, for instance, is used to weigh the prestige of the occasion. A major part of the money spent on celebration, which is usually borrowed, is reportedly for alcohol, and much of the motivation for this expenditure is the image surrounding how much alcohol is served at the function.

"We celebrated my sister's attainment very well. No-one in the village celebrated such an occasion in similar manner. We hired a cook. We also bought around sixty bottles of arrack and about seventy bottles of beer. People couldn't drink so much. It was too much for them. They started to pour the arrack on themselves. Some people slept throughout the whole night because they were so drunk. They left the following morning."

Our field assistant claims that nearly all youth in the village see this alcohol use as a sign of strength and status, almost a heroic thing. So they soon get into drinking. The field assistant thought that the villagers consider beating up the wife under the influence of alcohol as quite a normal occurrence. They sometimes reported such beatings in a way that suggested that it was an act to be proud of. The abuse sometimes led to marriages breaking up too.

Consequences of alcohol and other substance use

"Those who drink come home and start fighting with the wife and children. After all he is drunk isn't he? That's their nature when they are drunk."

The breaking up of marriages was referred to above. Children of these marriages may often end up in children's homes. This is not such a commonplace solution in any of the other settings that we sampled. A tendency to accept the 'dumping' of children in a children's home seems to prevail. In other settings members of the 'extended family' would more likely take on the upbringing of these children, most often the grandparents would provide shelter and care. Why this is less common in this community is not clear. It may simply be that the children of one broken family went in to a children's home and others in the community learnt of this option.

The economic burden from alcohol use is large. Other substances too compete with alcohol for significance of the economic burden. The majority of the villagers smoke cigarettes too, for example. Some claim they smoke as many as fifty cigarettes a day. Heroin use seems to have taken control of some people's lives even more than alcohol, and the economic drain from this is considered much more severe than that due to alcohol or tobacco.

"My husband is a drug addict. He earns about four hundred rupees a day. He gives about fifty to hundred rupees a day for household expenses. The rest he spends on drugs."

"When I'm with friends I don't realize how much I smoke. We usually smoke a few packets when we get together. It's almost impossible to keep count."

"When we smoke a cigarette, we always wonder how we are going to smoke another. But those who are addicted to heroin are not like that. They don't care about their wife and children. They don't think about providing for them. They even steal from the wife to buy drugs. They comb garbage dumps or steal a gold chain or something to find money to buy drugs."

Alcohol users said they drank to enjoy. They confirmed that it was indeed enjoyable when asked whether drinking alcohol was really enjoyable.

Changes over last few years

Despite the unpleasantness and problems that are seen and reported, there is still a feeling that the life in this community has changed for the better.

"People used to come to our village after doing an illegal thing or taking alcohol. Our village was a good place only for wrongdoers to hide, but things have changed. It is not like that now. Drug addicts are sent to different rehabilitation centres. Smoking is not a big problem. It is mainly heroin abuse."

3.4 An overcrowded residential setting II

The entry for data gathering in this setting, an urban community adjacent to Colombo, was different from that used in the overcrowded city setting described in the preceding section. Our field assistant used the 'informal entry' described at the beginning of this chapter and in the chapter on methodology. The same approach was used for the subsequent settings that are described in this chapter.

The overcrowded setting in Moratuwa is very different from that described previously. The environment is less obviously polluted. The air is cleaner and there are less flies and garbage. The municipality removes the garbage more often than in the other setting (where the garbage from elsewhere is dumped right beside the households!)

There is less fear of a sense of control by an unseen authority. The thugs or tough guys who control the cluster of houses ('village') are there to be seen. They get together and do things in a way that gives them attention. They don't often fight or interfere with other people's lives. Most of the time their social activity is to drink and make a noise among themselves. This can be in a small cul-de-sac where they will sit, but it is in a place where the others in the community can notice them and hear what they are discussing.

People share a lot of things. Our field assistant felt that even the idea of personal ownership of some things is very fluid. This is mostly due to lack of basic needs. There is a sense that things are collectively owned, even if there is an 'official' owner. A shirt that a young man owns will be used by his brother when he needs it for a particular purpose. The brother does not ask his permission to wear it, but simply takes it when he needs it. Such 'borrowing' can be from a 'brother' in another house too. The person in need of a shirt may be able, in some instances, to go to the house next door and get a shirt of his friend simply by informing the friend's mother that he is taking the shirt today.

The field assistant in the previous setting did not report this as a striking feature there. Whether this is due to his not having been struck by this particular aspect or because the realities are different in the two settings is not clear, but the sharing of essentials in a setting of deprivation looks very much like a coping or adaptation to lack of basic needs. It is mostly an expression of social or interpersonal solidarity.

Sharing may be of many things. Clothes, a camera, chairs, plates and glasses, jewellery, wristwatches, music cassettes and books and magazines are examples of things that can readily be 'borrowed' and returned. The borrowing is accepted and understood. The actual owner may not need to be consulted. If someone doesn't like this arrangement, he will need to make his feelings known and actively take steps to prevent his possessions being shared.

In some instances, underneath this all there is also a tinge of envy or unhappiness about someone who has more possessions than others. This amounts almost to jealousy, in the sense that the others will be resentful of this person's belongings. They may talk about it in a negative way. Sometimes the borrowing is a way of equalizing the possessions and not necessarily driven by a specific need or by sense of solidarity.

3.4.1 An example: Upali

Upali is in his forties, and he and his wife and two children are relatively happy. Their house is neat, but the things they have are not different from what the others have. They feel that others in the community don't like the fact that they have a relatively happy life.

"Although we have to let people borrow something in a time of need, there are some who ask things deliberately because they are unhappy about what we have. A few things can get lost or a camera may get broken, but is returned without a repair. How to refuse to lend things, without making enemies, requires special skills."

"Those who are unhappy with our having something more than them, are always the ones who earn more than us and waste it on various things. But they don't like us to save and buy something. They will find some way to get us to spend the same money that we would spend on alcohol or heroin if we were like them. It is especially two or three older men who make sure that we do what they want. They are in the habit, when they are drinking of shouting obscene words and making ugly allegations about people. If my wife does not give his wife some jewellery to wear when they are going on some special visit, I can guarantee that we will be abused some time in the next three days, when he is drunk."

"She may even lose the jewellery. Once we lost a chain. It was not very expensive, but still it had some value. The woman next door borrowed it, and she came back very upset and explained how it had got lost. They promised to pay, but I dare not remind them. This kind of thing keeps happening. I sometimes think that they do this deliberately because they don't like to see us better off than them. Everybody is jealous of us because we have no problems in our house and because I don't spend all my money on alcohol or heroin."

3.4.2 Another example: Chandana

Chandana is 24 years or so old. He lives in a crowded set of houses. He feels that there are 'no rules' about anything in his community. He is unmarried and lives with his parents.

'If you can get away with something, that is considered okay. Even to take something from your own household or your neighbour's, to steal or grab something from an unsuspecting stranger is all made acceptable'.

Chandana is clearly complaining about a feature that he recognized in his community. He is obviously unhappy. Whether his statement refers to real events or hypothetical ones, as illustrations, is not clear.

'I feel that every dirty thing begins in the alcohol setting. We allow people to say or do anything when they are drunk. Any dirty subject can be spoken openly, so it becomes part of accepted life in the community. For example someone will describe how an old lady's possessions were grabbed off her by a youth who pushed her onto the side of the road and ran away. In the drinking scene nobody wants to criticize this act.

Someone will say, 'So, how much did he get?' Then they make a joke about the amount being very small and express sympathy for the youth who got so little for his efforts'.

Here Chandana appears to be referring to an example from real life. The process he is referring to is probably not connected just with that particular event. A means of 'sanitizing' unacceptable behaviour by making it public appears to be at work. The perpetrator himself proclaims openly something he had done, which may well be against the norms in that particular setting or culture, but the uncritical acceptance of this 'confession' and the subsequent joking serves to make the act less unacceptable.

It is possible to see how the continued operation of this social dynamic can gradually make the previously unaccepted now accepted and later even admired. It is also possible to see how the process can apply to increasingly unacceptable behaviours. Such a process can hypothetically lead, given sufficient time, to a state where there may be nothing left that is considered unacceptable.

'Certain people in the community promote this kind of attitude in the drinking scene. Others don't disagree with them because they can become aggressive if you argue too much. So we keep quiet. Without even our realizing it their attitude or viewpoint becomes our norm too. (It becomes a normal thing or accepted thing – "Meka apeth eka wenawa"). Every nasty thing starts from or spreads from the drinking scene ("Hema jara ekakma enne bona thena indala patang arang"). From the drinking place these ideas and attitudes spread to the community's non-drinking life too'.

The alcohol serving and selling in this place is not one where people spend time. Illicit alcohol is bought and immediately consumed – with no opportunity to spend time conversing. Or people can take away their illicit brew in little polythene bags. There is little 'fun' associated with illicit alcohol use here. Somehow the 'fun' aspect of alcohol is restricted to settings where licit alcohol is consumed.

Why illicit alcohol users are not afforded the privilege of making the drinking a merry occasion, is unclear, but the phenomenon is not limited to this setting. The previous urban setting that we discussed, many of the village settings in our report and the 'Thotalanga' community of Sri Lanka (described in 'Illicit Alcohol' - Abeysinghe 2002) all seem not to allow 'fun' with illicit alcohol. People come, buy their kasippu and quickly drink it or carry it away.

What are the ingredients of 'enjoyment' in the alcohol setting? Is it simply that the poorest alcohol users drink 'kasippu', to cheaply fight off withdrawal symptoms? It is unlikely that enjoyment of alcohol is only a privilege of the rich. The poor too are allowed to drink and become noisy at community events where (licit) alcohol is served to the guests. They too become 'disinhibited' after alcohol use in these festivities.

The kasippu drinker too, even if he does not linger at the drinking setting, can shout abuse at people when he walks home drunk on alcohol. Perhaps the difference between licit and illicit alcohol effects on the 'fun' of drinking is that the seller does not provide facilities for people to sit around and 'enjoy' the drink. His business is, after all, illegal. When the setting does not provide facilities and cues for displaying 'enjoyment' the joy somehow disappears, it would seem.

Among young alcohol users there was the report that they did not drink daily and only used it to enjoy. When asked whether using alcohol was really enjoyable, nearly half of the informants here did not readily say it was. This is a great contrast with the previous urban overcrowded tenement that was described. Some of those here smiled in a slightly embarrassed way and said nothing. Others said it wasn't really so special. In the earlier urban tenement, on the other hand, nearly every male said alcohol was great and highly enjoyable.

The great similarity between this setting in Moratuwa and the previous overcrowded city community is in how people consume illicit alcohol. There is no expectation of social interaction around a bottle of kasippu. In fact most of it is sold in little polythene bags not bottles. No 'fun' is expected or achieved with illicit alcohol use.

Another similarity, striking and important, is the tendency to use the alcohol drinking occasion to weaken the power of social norms and feelings or right and wrong and of morality and decency. The open disclosure, sometimes with pride, of so called anti-social activities allows them eventually to be acceptable and permissible even in the non-drinking situation.

Equally striking is the difference in the way the alcohol experience was evaluated by younger persons in the two communities. In the first, alcohol use is rated universally to be highly enjoyable. In the second community, younger users are not all so convinced that it is indeed an enjoyable experience.

A commercial centre - Pettah

Pettah is the passenger transportation hub of Colombo. Buses to all parts of the country leave from here and so do trains. It is also a major commercial centre. Our field assistant says, 'There are three different worlds in this small area'.

Early morning is a bustle of getting organized for the day. People go to work early. Most of them are very active, alive and industrious. 'Nobody is spoilt (narak wela)'.

Daytime is a hive of tens of thousands in transit. A few workers who finish work by noon or so come to loiter in the 'crevices'. They spend time smoking, drinking and talking. Towards evening all the 'decent' folks rapidly disappear and get out – heading for home.

Night is a very different world. All the 'dredges' of society are left loitering. *'There is hardly anybody who is good, other than those waiting for the next available bus'*

Our field assistant spent time in Pettah sampling all of these 'worlds'. Much the largest amount of time (over ten days or so) was spent with the 'night world' of Pettah. He had no difficulty integrating with the setting. There are hardly any permanent people to talk to in Pettah, so our field assistant was immediately part of the setting as soon as he set foot there.

In the morning and daytime there are regulars – but they are all attending to their work and business, carrying things, setting things up for sale and trying hard to entice customers. They have little time to engage in 'small talk' with our field assistant, so conversation with them was limited to a few minutes each at most. It was not easy to get beyond issues of price of commodities on sale and times at which buses operated. Everybody was busy or on the move.

The night world was completely different. People were all ready to talk and eager to do so. Some of those who were around had finished work, but were hanging around waiting for the last bus instead of taking one that was immediately available. Many were openly consuming alcohol. This was done just standing around outside the bars. The bars had an equally heavy trade during the daytime, but the customers drank quickly and moved on. At night the customers hung around, walked about and kept coming back to base at the bar. Groups sat on the ground or road drinking alcohol – usually the cheapest arrack and not illegal alcohol. There were side settings that dispensed illegal alcohol to known regular customers, but they didn't sell in an obvious way.

The people who are around at night are very different from those seen during the day. They are 'down and out', not involved with anything productive, just walking the street and spending their time smoking and drinking alcohol with their regular clique or with any similar newcomer that they happen to meet. Gunapala is a clerk who works in a government department. He was at Pettah at 10.30 pm and was clearly after a few drinks – but he was not heavily intoxicated.

3.5.1 Example: Gunapala

'The last bus leaves at 11.30 so I will wait for that. There are more buses now, but I am not in a hurry to get home today. If I miss the last bus, I can sleep at the bus stand and go home tomorrow morning. I may just walk around and go home tomorrow morning, because I am not working tomorrow.'

Gunapala is not explicit about why he wants to loiter here. He is not forthcoming on whether home is so unpleasant that he has no wish to get there. Nor does he say that he finds the 'freedom' of just walking around the bus station and surroundings, doing anything he pleases and not answering to anybody a pleasant experience.

Among the people that Gunapala will see and mix with are lots of others who are waiting to get somewhere, but don't have a bus for some time. There are families and groups of girls too among those waiting. Gunapala can exchange a few words with them, loiter a little as someone himself waiting for a bus and rest his head somewhere briefly for a break.

Our field assistant judges that all of the regular folks who spend their late evenings and night at the bus stop and its surroundings are poor. Some of them have clerical jobs, but most of them have lesser-paid jobs. He guesses that the homes that they have to go to are probably abjectly poor. They are not all drinking heavily but they have all consumed at least some alcohol.

Gunapala in his government job has opportunities to earn money from people who come there to get work done. The work will get delayed if they don't pay someone something to make their job move. If Gunapala has a lucky day in the office, he may come to Pettah with an extra thousand rupees to spend.

'I don't get a lot of gifts from people often. Some days I 'get a chance'. Then we can all spend the money together here. If somebody else gets any money like that 'without trouble' they will spend it with friends.'

'I give some money from my salary to the family, but these people here have bought me food and drink when they had money – so I must treat them well when I get the chance'.

Gunapala has a wife and children, but prefers to spend the night walking the bus station than to go home. Somehow his home is not inviting enough.

He is a 'poor' man and has little money left in his pocket after alcohol expenses. Thus the deprived home setting may itself be a turn-off. Or he may be distanced from the family and able to find more convivial company among the 'friends' in Pettah. In Pettah he can remain anonymous even with the so-called friends, and he does not have to live up to a standard that may be expected in his home background. For example, he has to be the 'man' who provides the needs of the family, and when he is not able to deliver, there may be no way to show his masculinity through that criterion.

Even where the wife too does a job outside the home and earns money, the man is seen as the provider. The role of the man is to provide. A man who is unable to provide, may feel his masculine image a little under threat.

Pettah is the passenger transportation hub of Colombo. Buses to all parts of the country leave from here and so do trains. It is also a major commercial centre.

3.5.2 Example: Velu and Chaminda

Velu and Chaminda met our field assistant opposite the bar. They had their drinks and were now going home, and their train was due at around 7.15 p.m., they said. They started chatting to our field assistant at 7.00 p.m. and continued talking to him till 9.30 p.m., despite being reminded that they would miss the next train too. They have families, and one has a daughter too. Velu's sister is married to Chaminda and Chaminda's sister is married to Velu.

'They live near each other so it is alright if we get late. They have each other for company. We have terrible economic problems, and it is impossible to get out of this on our salaries, so we might as well spend the little we get enjoying today. We don't meet people like you every day, so we might as well stay and chat with you. We got our salaries yesterday so we can buy you a few drinks too.'

'The money we get is not enough even to turn around in a circle (rawumak kerakenna wath madi'), so what is the point? We might as well spend what we get for today's fun and see what happens tomorrow. Tomorrow is going to be terrible anyway'.

Nearly everybody who takes alcohol in Pettah says they do it for enjoyment or relaxation, and they confirm that the experience is indeed enjoyable when questioned whether alcohol was really a pleasant experience for them.

Again we see a contrast between the reported subjective experience of alcohol in Pettah and that reported by several users in the overcrowded urban community in Moratuwa. In Pettah the users of all ages say that they feel good with alcohol. Their subjective experience of being drunk is pleasant. This was the same as that reported from the first urban overcrowded setting described. The difference has something to do with the processing of alcohol use and its effects in these different settings rather than something to do with the research assistants. It was the same field assistant who got the positive report from Pettah and the negative from Moratuwa. The overcrowded tenement, where the experience of alcohol was rated as enjoyable by all, had a different field assistant.

Chaminda says,
'Well it's so good when we stay here and drink, because you can say or do what you like. Nobody to tell us that it is a bad thing or a sin. There are no rules'.

This may be what Chaminda finds enjoyable about alcohol and the alcohol setting or just Pettah at night. The rules that govern behaviour in the drinking setting in Pettah at night are different from what he recognizes as 'rules'. Perhaps the things that he calls rules are obligations. Here, with his friend and in-law Velu, he is not reminded of things that he has to do for his wife and children and others.

And Velu adds,
'We like to avoid unnecessary rules being put on us, even by our wives. We learn here how to live freely without rules. What we learn here we can remember at home also. If I see Velu in our home setting and we exchange a few words, then we remember something we discussed here and we act accordingly'.

'My wife may want some money for something for our child, but we may have decided to keep some extra earnings

The night world in Pettah is completely different. Some who finish work wait for the last bus instead of taking one that was immediately available. Many just 'hang around' smoking and drinking alcohol.

that we got, say from a bet, hidden from her. We may have planned to spend it with friends tomorrow, and I may be persuaded to part with some of this money when my wife asks and I see my child, but then I go to meet Chaminda and have a word with him. He strengthens my mind again and reminds me what we decided here in Pettah earlier. Then I am strong enough again to keep the money hidden from my wife'.

The rules that Chaminda was complaining about become clearer with Velu's account. It is mostly to do with having to support the family, or being obliged to support the family. There is an undertone of not 'obeying' your wife. Once again this reflects the issue of masculinity and the role of the man in the family. Among the men in Pettah a different view of the man is propagated. The man does not do what the wife says or wants. He keeps out of her reach and keeps company with men and enjoys men's fun.

These appear to be men who cannot win in the struggle to show their masculinity by providing conspicuously – or even by providing adequately. They may be resorting to membership in a 'men's club' to reinforce the idea of their masculinity.

Here too, what happens in the alcohol setting appears to spill over to the non-drinking time. (This reflects in a different way what the man in Moratuwa said, (*'I feel that every dirty thing begins in the alcohol scene'*). Velu here is not giving an account of something that he feels is bad, but the values within the alcohol scene has clearly spilled over to the rest of his life, and the fact that it influences the quality of his family life too is evident.

Chaminda and Velu are not very complementary about the others in their community who do not consume alcohol.

'All they care about is money. What is the point of carefully collecting money when you know that life is uncertain? They just want to show that they are superior. They love to show off their possessions. That is why they are so miserly about spending some money with friends or on enjoying life. People who don't drink are misers and only want to show that they are superior to the others, but only they think so. Everybody in the village knows that they are stingy misers.'

'If we have a problem and my wife asks for some support until I get some money, they will pretend that there is no money in the house. When I ask, they can find the money that was not there when my wife asks! We should not allow such misers to prosper.'

The hostility to those who are less badly off than themselves is evident here, and there is almost a justification put forward to bring the better off persons down. *'We should not allow such misers to prosper'*. If they don't spend their money on alcohol as much as these two persons, they are misers and want to show that they are superior to others. Not only do Chaminda and Velu claim that the better off non-users of alcohol should not be allowed to prosper – they have even found a way to do so. When they ask for money from the people who told their wives that they don't have any, somehow the money appears.

We heard in previous accounts that in settings where there are many poor homes crowded together there is little scope for one family to rise above the rest. Most of these accounts appeared to be from the point of view of people who would like to 'develop' but were unable to do so in their setting. Chaminda and Velu provide a different slant. They are close to the thinking that others should not be allowed to develop or to overtake them. They provide reasons to keep the others down and happily provide an example of how they make others who may prosper to part with money, probably unwillingly.

The cooperative shop

An unusual source of data gathering emerged in this setting. Our regular field assistant linked up with an employee of this shop in order to get an introduction to the shop. But it wasn't easy for a researcher to mingle for long in a shop, without buying something and leaving. As a result we eventually asked our first informant, who was an employee of the shop, to be the field assistant and gave him the necessary guidance for a while. So the account below is through a regular member of the community itself, operating also as our field assistant. A great deal of bias is therefore likely, despite the regular supervision.

3.6.2 Example: Malinie

A lady, say 'Malinie', working in a 'Cooperative shop' in Colombo has a daughter who is 13 years old. When this daughter 'attains age', or has her first menstrual period, much has to be done in a hurry. The parents have to find a lot of money in one go, often quite suddenly. 'We have to do our best for our daughter. She's our only daughter'. The lady borrows a lot of money for the festivities and rituals. The amount usually exceeds the annual salary. Malinie borrowed less, Rs 50,000, from her work colleagues and many others. They don't charge an interest but give out of friendship – and they know that she will pay them back soon through a loan, against her salary, that she can get from her employer.

The staff working in this shop seem here to be showing a real sense of solidarity. In many instances money is given on interest and there are several avenues for doing so. The fact that Malinie's workmates are willing to give money like this is therefore an expression of real or genuine solidarity. They can trust her to return the loan because they work together and she will find it hard to renege.

'Cooperatives' are stores that sell a wide variety of household provisions, rather like a supermarket. They are government owned and run. Most of the time these establishments fail to make a profit, but they continue to run because the government bears the loss.

Malinie's husband takes as much responsibility as she does, or even more, to get the necessary funds for this event. This is probably true for the majority of husbands in families of this social group, whether the wife works in a job outside the home or not. For a few women though, the husband will not be a great support financially, but most of these husbands too would still help in the numerous things that have to be done.

We do not know how much Malinie's husband raised, compared to what she did. Whatever the amount, the situation for the village wife is quite the opposite.

A village woman whose daughter 'attains age' has to go through the same rituals and festivities. She has to engage her husband's participation and cooperation with more effort. If she is lucky the husband will provide the money for the festivities. Far more often than in the city though, he will not, or will not be able to, provide. The things to be done are similar for both settings. Determining the correct time to bath the daughter (after which she re-emerges, having been kept out of sight of males) is, for instance, done by astrologers.

The lady in the village too has to borrow money. Since she has no friends who can loan money and no loans available from her employers, she pays interest, usually at 10 – 15 % per month or so. The same solidarity that Malinie had from her friends at the workplace is not usually enjoyed by the woman in the village, and she too has to celebrate the event as much as the city-woman – or maybe even more.

There has to be a party, whether the event happens in the city or the village. Malinie and her husband invite their friends and relations to it. Quite a large number of invitees are from their workplaces. Half of the money raised by Malinie (50,000 rupees) is spent on alcohol for the guests. "We don't want people to laugh at us."

The mother in the village is concerned that people will not even give the gifts they bring if there is not enough alcohol. This does not appear to be a great concern for Malinie. She has not heard of people taking back the money that they brought for a gift, on the ground that alcohol was not served or that the amount of alcohol served was inadequate.

The money Malinie borrowed is paid back to the friends at her workplace through a loan she gets from her employer (i.e., the government). She does not use the gifts given by friends who come to the party, to repay her loans. The gifts were mostly cash, and came to more than rupees 100,000. Part of that money is put into the daughter's bank account (Rs 50,000), and the rest spent to buy a computer for the daughter and sons.

The monthly deduction from her salary is a significant reduction of income. They have great difficulty managing day to day expenses now. She does borrow money to meet monthly expenses, but again free of interest and to be paid back from the next salary. The small salary left after deduction of the loan repayment is further dwindled by repayment of that month's borrowings from colleagues.

Malinie sees that her financial state is precarious. She has no regrets about the loan and the costs incurred. 'At least my daughter has 50,000 rupees to call her own, and nobody can say we didn't have a proper party for her coming of age'. If things get really bad, she'll have to see how to manage – but she will not disturb the savings in her daughter's account. She'll have to borrow money on interest, as a last resort. Malinie is not too fearful that this may happen. She thinks her husband will come up with a solution. He is a government employee too, but there are ways for him to earn extra cash.

If she is really stuck, she still has some jewellery to pawn to a bank or a financing institution (pawning centre). The interest that the bank or the pawning centre charges is much less than that of the 'sharks'.

Malinie, despite her loans and other financial difficulties appears to be better off than two other ladies in the shop. (But they still lend her money!) She has a bigger house than them and has good furniture. This appears to be a cause for discontent too. The other ladies are critical of her life and often say some nasty things about her in her absence. The impression is that the others are jealous of her higher economic status. There is less jealousy about her among the more junior grades than among the ones at her level. They often laugh at the sources of her income, and imply that her husband earns money by soliciting bribes from people who come to his office to get work done.

From the account of Malinie's daughter's event we can see that the undertone of envy is not completely absent even in this setting, where there appeared to be much greater solidarity and friendship than in some other settings that we studied. The shop as a whole offers a contrast with the more obviously poor and deprived groups that were focused upon in the other accounts. There are people in the shop whose earnings are much less than that of the village family, but they still appear to be less abjectly poor than the village person with the same or slightly higher income.

3.6.2 Example: Sanjeewa

Day-to-day life for 23 year old Sanjeewa, working in the same 'Cooperative Shop' as Malinie, has a pattern of life fixed by the job he does. He can tell us exactly what he will be doing on any day that we pick – even three months away. 'What will you be doing on Tuesday the 25th of March 2003?' we may ask him in January. He will say 'I shall get home at about 9.00 a.m. because my night shift is on Mondays. I will eat, wash and so on and sleep until about 4.00 p.m. Then, after eating something that my mother has cooked and left for me for lunch, I have to wash all my accumulated soiled clothes. I go to my friend Jagath's house almost every Tuesday because on other days I have no time. I will chat with him and a friend of his who is boarded in their house until about 8.30 or so. We will usually have a cup of tea that Jagath's younger sister serves us. We will watch TV together with Jagath's family. I will then go home and eat the dinner that my mother has prepared and immediately go to bed, because I have to leave for work early on Wednesday.

What he does on special holidays is relatively fixed too. These are holidays that happen about once a month. These are days for enjoyment. There is some official public holiday at least once a month, and there are often public events organized somewhere in the city. These events are well publicized through the media station that is usually a co-sponsor. Sanjeewa will always attend one of these open-air musical shows if it is within reasonable distance. Three colleagues from his workplace and Jagath and his friend all join him.

Whether Sanjeewa is really upset or unhappy about his highly regular life is not too clear, but the musical show is most likely a welcome break form routine. Ironically, the break is routinized too. Alcohol, with the social trappings implying freedom or 'time out' probably serves to add to the value of this event as a break from routine.

Sanjeewa is a 'minor employee' at the cooperative shop. He takes home about rupees 4,800 every month. The only 'enjoyment' that he believes he has is the one day of fun. Or rather, the one evening and night. So he spends whatever is necessary. Usually he and his friends each spend over Rs 1,000 on such an evening. Most of the costs are for alcohol. Beer is sold at the venue, so are cigarettes. More expensive items are spirits. 'The best experience is with lemon gin. It gives a much greater euphoria ('somiyak', 'aathal ekak'). Lemon gin is much more expensive that the usual arrack. They buy it and drink outside or carry it to the premises of the musical show.

Consumption of 'lemon gin' has to be made visible to all. It highlights a month's or year's special evening, and a great deal of discussion of the cost and the kick of lemon gin occurs forever after. Conversation in the shop somehow reverts to the occasion when this particular alcohol was consumed.

For Sanjeewa the occasional day on a weekend like this is fun, an enjoyment of life. All other days are boring, monotonous and unpleasant, as he sees it.

Sanjeewa likes to have the right clothes for these events and is not very happy with what he can afford. Another man, Thilak, in the same shop knows the current fashions more than the others. He always buys the newest style shoes and the best jeans. Sanjeewa does not know how this guy is so well informed about fashions, but Thilak is from a wealthier family than the others. Thilak is a cashier and so earns more than them in the shop too. The cashier has a higher salary than Sanjeewa and has other ways of earning 'extra' on the side. This is most easily done by not issuing a receipt for customers who are in a hurry.

There are no strong norms about clothes. Most of the younger employees learn what to wear by copying each other, but they may not succeed in being 'really' fashionable the way Thilak is. It is not easy to conform to that level of fashionability. It is that of a slightly wealthier social class. Conformity with that group can more readily be achieved by drinking, even occasionally, special brands of alcohol.

Older 'minor employees' of the shop have to run a family on Sanjeewa's income. It is less than that of most poor people in a village, but they still appear less poor than the poor village person, as long as they do not reside in a 'slum'. This impression needs to be checked out more carefully. If it is indeed the case, how this comes about is worth investigating.

3.6.3 The setting in general

The twenty or so employees of the shop get on well with each other and the organization is not highly regimented. Higher rankers are called 'Madam' or 'Sir' but the first name is attached sometimes – 'Malinie Madam'. In some settings the higher officials are not accessible to the lower grades, but here the structure is small and the lowest paid employee too gets to talk to the lady manager as a normal part of work. The chief is a woman not a man. This is not common.

Money

All grades of employee depend almost entirely on their salary for survival. If the salary stopped, about three-fourths of the staff would have a hard time surviving even a month. When the salary comes, it comes already with a deduction of loan instalments. So most people already begin

When people are asked about the cost of the alcohol they consume, the answer is based on the actual amount they purchase and drink. Donations for others' alcohol is not usually added. Those who get alcohol free do not add this to the reported cost of their alcohol consumption either.

the month 'behind' on their regular salary, and then there are loans to pay off to friends at the office itself and to others outside. These are settled on pay-day itself. About ten employees participate in a 'seettu' where each one puts in 500 rupees and the money goes to one person in rotation. The organizer of the seettu gets the option of taking the first month's collection.

People talk a lot about money matters and the cost of living. Money certainly is an important determinant of wellbeing and life for those earning the relatively low salaries of the shop. When financial difficulties arise, it is mostly the single men working at the shop who have to give loans to the married men, and sometimes to the women. Nobody has so far experienced a refusal, or significant delay, in getting their money back, but it is almost like a permanent loan, as the borrower comes back for a loan within a week or so. The 'chronic borrower' consumes alcohol rather heavily.

One of the men spends over half of his salary on tobacco and alcohol, but not on other drugs. He comes after a drink of alcohol in the morning too. Pilferage and stealing probably occurs, according to some of the staff, but not the majority. Nobody talks about who is stealing or making money on the side. There are no identified 'bad characters' who do not belong to the general staff community. If, say, a cashier is suspected of pocketing for himself the money from sales where a receipt is not issued, nobody talks about it. Nor does anybody else ask for a share of the spoils. The absence of open discussion of this possibility may reflect solidarity. On the other hand it may be due to uncertainty over who really does steal and who does not.

The lowest paid in the shop does not 'look' poorer than the highly paid, but they may be managing life precariously. The visible level of affluence of the different levels of staff at the shop doesn't really reflect any obvious difference based on their level of income. The life circumstances of the lowest income earners do not sound too deprived. People have visited each other's houses, and the homes of the lowest income earners are not described in a way suggestive of significant deprivation or overt 'poverty'.

Conversation

After money matters, most conversation is about what happens in television dramas. Politics, cricket and gossip about each other all figure in conversation. Men, especially the single men, tend to talk about their fun experiences. Nearly all of these centre around alcohol consumption, and the most fun events are presented as those with the most alcohol. They occasionally brag about their sexual exploits, but not with specific details narrated. This kind of narration happens in men-only situations when some of them get together for some 'fun', and then take alcohol. To brag about sexual activities is probably a masculine norm generally, and not necessarily a feature limited to this setting.

Alcohol

Alcohol use among the staff as a group is mainly in the event of a celebration or party in one of the homes of a staff member. In these events the amounts consumed by members of the office staff (other than by one individual) is not very large. Even the person who drinks a lot behaves in a very 'civilized' way during these events, but they do talk a lot after the event about the alcohol they consumed, even though it was not a key event in the evening. The use of alcohol by the female members of staff is talked about much more than that of the males.

A much more significant part is played by alcohol in the lives of the members of the staff in their men-only drinking occasions. These are with people outside of the office, but rarely is there a report of aggression, violence or 'misbehaviour' after alcohol use, even from these events. The drain on people's earnings is mostly through parties, events or celebrations that they attend or have to host themselves.

When asked, very few of the occasional users said that they enjoyed alcohol intoxication. They all said that they drank to conform, but it wasn't clear how nearly all could claim to be drinking to conform, and not for enjoyment of the alcohol use *per se*. The field assistant was asked to raise this question. The answers were almost defensive. If nearly all find alcohol use not a really enjoyable experience and nearly all were drinking to conform, what was the force that made alcohol use the 'conformist' behaviour? Some appeared not to understand the question, but others said that it was the done or expected thing. The implied answer is that the feeling that one should take alcohol in fun situations came from the environment – not necessarily from among the members of the group.

One possible explanation for most occasional users reporting that they did not enjoy the effect of alcohol is that they felt that our informant 'wanted' that answer. This would be particularly likely if the informants were somehow giving cues that they did not approve alcohol use, but our informant in this case was not a complete teetotaler, and not heavily biased against alcohol use. If at all his bias would have been in the opposite direction. This we would have needed to explore if the answers were in the opposite direction.

There are some unusual features of this setting, compared to others. Firstly there is only one person who definitely consumes much alcohol daily. A second person probably drinks daily. The 'negative' behaviours of overt aggression and abuse are not common in their drinking occasions, and poverty is not so obvious even among those who earn very small salaries.

This is a more 'middle class' story, it appears. The norms are of the middle class. In income, the average for the shop is probably close to the average income of 'poor' families that we described in relation to the others settings. Somehow, in identity, the people here appear to align themselves with the norms of the better off. Not making scenes of overt aggression and violence after alcohol use is an example. The quiet acceptance of the open sipping of alcoholic beverages by women folk, at parties, is another. The use of alcohol by women is almost a sign of 'not belonging to the village'.

Boarding life

Our field assistant befriended several young men living in rented premises or 'boardings' through casual conversation, and follow up of such meetings. In several instances he asked for details of places where he could find lodging, in case he too may have to find alternative accommodation soon. He then continued to make visits to these boardings where he made closer linkages. He would have spent about twelve days (mostly late evenings) conversing and participating in the life of the persons of that particular boarding.

The 'boarding' is the village people's home in the city. Those who are too far to travel to and from work daily must have a place to live within closer reach of the workplace. These boardings are of different sizes and varieties. There are two aspects of boarding life. On the one hand it is a home away from home, so there is the possibility of living by different norms from the village. A greater sense of freedom, an absence of social control, prevails. The other aspect is that boarding life is somehow not 'real'. Life is suspended and really begins only when one sets foot on home soil, but a greater part of the month is spent in the less real reality.

Some boarders take a room in a house where the resident family rents out a part for extra income. Four persons, on average, share a small room. There is usually a toilet (outside the main house) and a place for washing and bathing. In other 'boardings' all the rooms are for lodgers and the person who owns the building visits to check things and to collect the rent. These houses may have 20 or more people living in them.

We even encountered a 'boarding' house with 80 men living in it, but could not obtain adequate access during the time available. This was run by the employer of the residents – who all worked in shifts in his sales outlets. Our field assistant did make friends with people in several other boardings and visited them daily in the evenings. There are differences between boardings, but the similarities are more striking.

3.7.1 Example: Gemunu

Gemunu is 19 and works as a 'barber' in a hairdressing saloon. His boarding has six others living in it. He is the youngest and most recent resident. Boarding 'life' really begins when the majority return from work each day. One of the six is much more influential than the others.

'Priyantha Aiya has been here for over two years now. The owners of the house expect him to make sure that we all behave properly – in a way that will not be a problem for them. Priyantha Aiya knows everybody in the locality. So it is very useful for us that he is here. He introduced me to the house from where he gets his meals and they give me my meals too. It is so convenient because the food is cheaper than at a hotel, cleaner and available every day even if I get a little late.'

The culture of each boarding is dependent on the nature of the person or persons who are most influential. In some the 'aiya' (elder brother) is more strict and demanding. Others have to do small favours for him. In others, the influential members are extremely helpful and look after the rest like they were members of their own family.

'Luckily for us Priyantha Aiya is very helpful and looks after our interests. He advises us when we are out late. He doesn't smoke and doesn't allow anyone else to smoke in the room. Sometimes he joins us for a trip to a musical show, and he will drink just one beer. And we don't drink much when he is there'.

The characterization of another senior in a boarding is very different.

3.7.2 Example: Thusitha

Thusitha lives in a boarding, which he found through Wickrama who works in the same factory. Wickrama told Thusitha when he came to work that he lived in a boarding very conveniently located for the workplace. He said that he would get a place there for Thusitha too, so Thusitha left the room he had and joined this boarding in one month. Thusitha's account contrasts a good deal with Gemunu's.

"Wickrama Aiya is respected in the factory. He always speaks up about any issue in the factory. Other workers tend to listen to Wickrama Aiya. We don't have a trade union, but the management also talks to Wickrama Aiya when there is a small problem. He usually solves it for them, so I don't want to leave this boarding that Wickrama Aiya has found.

Often I have to buy cigarettes for him. He always runs out of money. Most times he forgets to give me the money later. When we go out for an evening, the others contribute more than Wickrama. He pulls out all the his money in his pocket and gives it, but it is generally less than the cost of what he has consumed, and we have to bear the cost of his transport back too. Nobody complains about this system."

The more senior persons in the boardings are usually married and have to send money home regularly. Wickrama has a wife and children to support. Younger men who are single have commitments to their parents and brothers and sisters who often depend on them. Even those who have to support families in this way are persuaded to contribute more than their share of expenses for shared 'entertainment' activities of the group.

"They will say that I am not married and so can afford to spend more than them. This is not like a forceful demand – but I feel shy not to spend when they say that. They say that they spent on all their friends parties and alcohol before they got married."

This theme of forcing or persuading others to subsidize the alcohol expenses of those who consume most is seen in many other settings. If a person is asked the cost of the alcohol he consumes, he gives the cost of the alcohol that he himself purchases and consumes. What others pay for is not accounted for in the calculation. Those who pay for others' alcohol do not add this to their reported 'alcohol expenses' either. A large part of alcohol expenditures is hidden in this way.

For some of the younger members the cost of subsidizing others entertainment (mostly alcohol) is large. They sometimes gladly pay the bill when the crowd goes out for fun, and most of the bill is for alcohol. Very few have expenses other than for food and clothes and travel. Not much is left for clothes. For some this can be a weekly expense. They like to support their parents if they can, but often the money is spent. They still go home once a month or so to see their family, and some have to get money from their home to get back to work.

'Even if I was living at home my parents still had to spend to give me food. Now the only benefit of doing a job is that they don't have to pay for my needs. Sadly, I still have to take money from them to survive in Colombo, even while doing a job. Still I am less of a burden to them than when I was living unemployed at home.'

Some of the young members have girl friends. Then they have to spend on them also. If they go out, the evening's (or day's) total cost can be considerable. There is no place with much privacy for a couple to spend time together. Sometimes they rent a room in a hotel, but this is in the range of 500 rupees or so even for a few hours.

'Although I may not join the boarding friends to go out for fun on a day that my girl friend is free, I am still asked to join the group. If they are short of money for their evening, they will ask me to contribute a little, so I have to spend for all the things with my girlfriend and still give a little money to the friends who are going out drinking without me.'

Not everybody gives money like this. They are not threatened to give money, but pressurized to do so. Some of those who want to be 'popular' may be more prone to make contributions like this. Those who do not wish to contribute, are allowed to refrain from doing so, but they are made to feel that they are not good members of the group. They are 'unpopular', labelled misers and criticized in their absence. Any newcomer soon learns what he must do to avoid acquiring the same image as these unpopular members of the boarding.

'It is as you get gradually more senior in the boarding that you start drinking alcohol or taking tobacco. When a newcomer arrives in some boardings, the others will assault him physically for a trivial reason. In such boardings the older group keeps a lot of authority, and this is the way they do it. Any word or remark that the person says is enough to provoke a more senior person or two to hit him, but they don't go on assaulting after that. The others teach the newcomer how he should behave and comfort him, but he learns that there are people in the boarding who should be 'respected'. He may never again be assaulted physically, and the person who hit him may even indicate that he is sorry. 'I shouldn't have been angry for the small thing you said' he may say.'

Whether this ensures regular participation in group activities of the 'boarding' is not clear. It is almost like an 'initiation' in some boardings to be physically attacked for some trivial reason, at least once. This occurs soon after the person takes up residence, and is quickly brushed aside by the others who tell him not to take it too seriously. 'He's not always like that, but sometimes he loses his temper'.

Large numbers travel home at weekends from city 'boardings' (hostels) where they reside to work or study. So much that is new is learnt in the city and instantly transferred to the village.

A system of compulsory savings occurs in some boardings. All those who contribute have to pay a fixed amount every month to this 'seettu'. The total is handed to one person each month based on the luck of a draw. The organizer of the seettu gets the first month's collection. This system, according to many, is the only way to save any money. If people try to save money in a bank or in some other way, there is no pressure to keep up the payments. In a seettu there is no hope of avoiding payment, so money gets automatically saved, but there are risks, because people can lose their job and move away. So 'seettus' are generally among long-term residents in stable jobs.

Seettu money can also go for a celebration, for alcohol and special activities, but most seettu money is utilized 'productively'. Some item of furniture for the house, repairing a roof or getting a TV set are examples of things done with seettu money. Nobody in the boardings visited had mobile telephones, which is surprising. Young people especially like mobile phones to show off as a sign of success. Boardings were perhaps too insecure to keep a mobile phone for long without losing it. A few at the boarding had wristwatches, and all of these were of less than four hundred rupees or so in value.

There was an impression among some that people invested in few such possessions not only because these could easily get lost. Nobody wanted to appear better off than the others. This they felt could invite jealousy and create problems for them from a few individuals in the boarding.

'If they felt that I had more money than them, some would be unhappy. Especially Prasanna. And he will pass hints and be unpleasant then if I refused to make a contribution to something. I save money in a savings account, but I don't keep the book here as they will all definitely study it carefully. The others who show they are friendly will also be jealous if they see that I have some savings'.

The theme of envy and jealousy, even among the relative strangers that come together in a boarding is again visible. The image of even slightly greater affluence than the others will invite hostility. This idea had come up repeatedly. Whether the feeling of envy is a social characteristic of the entire nation or only of the relatively poorer segments of society that were mostly sampled here, is not clear.

The three-wheeler stand

Three-wheelers are parked everywhere, but these parking places are really 'stands' where there is a cluster of regulars. A person with a three-wheeler cannot just go and park somewhere until a 'hire' comes along. He (our research assistant did not find a single woman among the three-wheeler drivers) has to belong to a particular spot. Newcomers have to get a place through the sponsorship of someone already a part of a particular stand.

Our field assistant found it easy to mix and get into conversation with the men at these stands. The drivers were completely unoccupied and had little to do between 'hires', so they readily spoke with the field assistant who was loitering with them.

The most striking feature that our field assistants report is that in many of the stands with which they engaged there were people with links to criminal, shady or 'borderline' activities. These were usually the larger stands in crowded centres.

Most of the drivers who park their vehicles (three-wheelers) had these on hire and paid the owner of the vehicle 250 to 300 rupees per day, they said. The driver had to meet the cost of fuel. His income after these expenses ranged from two to six hundred rupees per day. The average earnings of the majority are between eight to fifteen thousand rupees per month.

Not all drivers were at this level of earning. Some had other 'side-businesses' that earned them much more, but quite a few lived in relatively deprived home settings, as could be gathered from clues in their conversation. Even those who earned relatively large amounts felt that they could not emerge from poverty while they resided in the places in which they now lived. The explanation for this is not very clear.

A few three-wheeler drivers are rich. They need not waste their time driving people around for a hire, but they keep the job because it is their avenue for other 'side' income. Some of this side income is not quite legal or decent, according to their own description. There are drivers probably engaged in bigger criminal activities or networks.

'Peter's gold chain and bracelet are more expensive than his new three-wheeler. He doesn't need to sit here waiting for a fifty-rupee hire, but his other income is dependent on being in this business'.

So there are individuals or groups who are part of some other money-making network. They may help a rich person find sexual partners and deliver these partners too. They may be lookouts or informants for criminals. They may even be transporting heroin or handguns or bombs. All of these require that they drive the three-wheeler as their job. These individuals have more power than others in the 'stand'.

The powerful person in the stand is the person who has more criminal contacts or knows more ways of earning money. There will be one person who knows a foreign resident in the area, or a rich man. He provides services specially to this client.

If the foreign gentleman wants something done, he will contact the driver whom he knows, and that driver's stature grows. He can provide a sex worker to a lucrative client and get favours in return. If he is unable to attend to a special client, he will entrust the client only to someone else from the stand, whom he picks carefully.

The economic status of all the drivers is similar except for an individual or two. They have become like that through some powerful connection or illegal business. Others don't criticize or get in the way of these 'aiyas' (elder brothers), but among the rest there is the feeling that all must be similar and one person can't 'overtake' the others.

'Even though we are friends and support each other against outsiders, there is a lot of jealousy of each other too. I can save enough money if I manage things properly to buy my own three-wheeler in about two years, but I am never able to save. I don't know how it happens, but the others don't let me save. They make sure that I spend on the same things that they waste their money on.'

The night-time stand and daytime stand are completely different. In the late evenings the daytime drivers are replaced by different individuals. There is less of a 'community' in the night setting. Several of the drivers sit in their own three-wheeler and do not mix with the others. In the daytime they rarely sit alone. This is partly because it is so hot in the daytime, our field assistant speculates. They have to go to a shade if the vehicle is parked in the hot sun. This forces people together. In the evenings and night, they can be comfortable sitting in their own vehicle.

The people who drive are also different. The daytime drivers live somewhere nearby and go home at night. Quite a few of the night drivers are people from 'outstations' (namely, people whose homes are elsewhere and who lodge in Colombo for employment). Several of them do a daytime job too and drive the three-wheeler at night, for additional income. There is less 'shady' business carried out by this group. The drivers are mostly from a different way of thinking, and the police too are more vigilant at night. A three-wheeler driver is more likely to be stopped and questioned by the police in the night than in the daytime.

There is a culture that evolves in each three-wheeler stand peculiar to itself, but our field assistants felt that the similarities were remarkable. And the 'three-wheeler stand' culture is more relevant to the daytime group than to the night group. It is they who mix with each other, socialize and share things, and often live in close proximity to each other. Their homes are close to the 'stand', so their social setting included the area of the stand even before they became three-wheeler drivers.

What happens in the three-wheeler stand is therefore a reflection of life in the communities from which those who drive these vehicles come. These are overcrowded poor communities. When something happens in anybody's home, the community is instantly aware of it, and the three-wheeler stand too becomes a place in which this can be discussed. How people behave and should behave is discussed and decided in the stand too.

Our research assistants found it easy to mix and get into conversation with the men at three wheeler stands. The drivers were completely unoccupied and had little to do between 'hires'

3.8.1 Example: Jayantha

Jayantha's daughter attained age recently. He is now in trouble trying to settle the expenses that were connected to the ceremony related to her coming of age. Jayantha thinks that the money could have been better spent, instead of being lavishly wasted at a party, but he acknowledges that he had no choice in the matter. He says privately that he would not have been allowed to avoid having a big party.

Not having a party for his daughter's 'attaining age' would have caused a stir in their community in which he lived. People would have, he feels, asked him or 'ordered' him to have one. This includes the friends he meets daily at work at the stand.

'If I said I was not having a party, the others would have said that they would organize it for my daughter, so there would have been a party whether I wanted it or not, and my daughter would have been ashamed'.

Who will 'not allow' not having a party? *'Everybody'*.

It transpires that 'everybody' specially includes his wife's parents and a few vociferous individuals in the crowded neighbourhood in which he lives. There is one person in the three-wheeler stand too, who would have insisted that he throw a party. Jayantha points out one of his friends there.

'If Peiris there realized that I was not going to have a big party, he would personally have almost ordered me to do so. He lives close to my home and knew about the event, so he and the others automatically assume that we are hurriedly organizing every thing for the party, and they will offer help. I have no chance of refusing'.

How can Peiris order Jayantha to have a big party for his daughter's event?
"It's not just Peiris. He would have just taken the lead. All the others too would have agreed with him. He would have said to the others, 'Machan this guy is trying to avoid his responsibilities towards his family. Why don't we get together and give this sweet girl the celebration she deserves?' And they could have done it too. I of course did want to give a party, so they didn't have to do this. I am only guessing what they may have done. I was just trying to imagine what would have happened because you asked me."

It transpires that Peiris also has the habit of shouting loudly and becoming abusive when he walks home heavily intoxicated. If he has felt some grudge against anybody, that person will be vilified by him in public abuse. He may make ugly allegations of sexual misconduct or stealing about the person that he is annoyed with. In the morning Peiris does not recall these events and does not have to feel embarrassed when he confronts the person that he abused the previous evening. He will greet and talk to the person as if nothing had happened.

Jayantha is not frightened that Peiris can physically abuse him, but he would not want to risk the verbal abuse that Peiris is capable of, when intoxicated. Not many people in the village would, either.

3.8.2 Poverty

Somehow, the majority of three-wheeler drivers are poor. They appear to live in difficult circumstances. This is partly because they have to earn daily and live on it. If they have a good day, the money goes in some way or another. Nothing remains for the next day. If they have a bad day, money has to be found from some source on the basis of repayment with tomorrow's earnings. It is usually possible to get this without payment of interest from another three-wheeler driver.

Opportunities or a 'chance' happens from time to time. Someone may forget a parcel or leave something of value. An inexperienced client may be unexpectedly generous. On days where good fortune strikes, the others feel entitled to a share. This means entertaining them at the end of the day. The lucky person doesn't always keep his good luck a secret. He seems to be happy to spend it all on the others that evening. It is almost a matter of pride. Such unexpected windfalls appear not to be regarded as 'real' income, so it is okay to spend it all in the evening. The easiest way to spend it is to celebrate with friends, and the commonest celebration is to drink lots of alcohol.

In several three-wheeler stands the group of drivers tend to socialize after work with one another, and with a few others who loiter with them at the stand. There may be more than one 'clique' like this, but there was no evidence of hostility between the different cliques. Our field assistants felt that the clique had a strong say on how a driver spent his leisure time. If the others wanted to quit, he would stop work too even if there were hires available.

3.8.3 Alcohol

Many of the cliques have members who wanted to take quite a bit of alcohol every day, before going home. Others too would be invited to join them. Some would join on special days even if they were not keen on drinking. A special day would be any day where a few would propose to have a party. There doesn't have to be a special reason for these regular events. If they haven't all gone out drinking for several days that means they'd go out today. If any member of the clique gets an unexpected sum of money, then they all have to go out in the evening. (It would often still be inadequate for all the evening's expenses, but the others would have to put in less than on the usual 'evening out'.

'Let's get together for some fun this evening. (Why don't we get set this evening?) Sarath has got a good break today and he wants to give us a good time.'

On such evenings all the members of the clique would join in 'having fun'. It would be different from the routine of the regular daily drinkers. They would not just drink some alcohol and go home, but would linger and spend time drinking and socializing together. There would be things to eat alongside the drinking. No member of the clique could avoid joining these special occasions, and they could be more than once a week. Thus all members were obliged to consume alcohol more than once a week.

They would have to consume alcohol whether they wished to or not. Nobody refused, and probably nobody wished not to consume either.

'If we go out for fun, then it means we also want to have fun like the others. So there is no reason for anybody to be forced to consume. If we did not like to drink, would we go out with these friends?'

Other than relative newcomers to that place nearly all the members of a clique take alcohol in the evening. It is not easy to stay separate from this culture, and the newcomers too get into more frequent use rather quickly. Overall the economic impact of alcohol purchasing alone was very high for this group. Lost revenue due to stopping work early on days that were for 'enjoyment' was another form of economic drain. A member of the setting who is not a regular heavy drinker says,

'These people earn 10,000 to 15,000 rupees a month and they have only about 4,000 to 5,000 rupees really to spend on their families'.

In these drinking sessions they talk about the day's experiences. Some of these relate to unexpected opportunities that arose that day. Newcomers learn in these boasting sessions what is possible to do. They learn that some things are matters to be proud of.

'A colleague will say how he noticed a girl who seemed to be waiting for somebody and not being sure what to do when the person does not turn up. The new guy has not even realized what has happened. This person goes up to the girl and starts talking to her and warns her not to loiter there too long as it is not a good place for a girl to be alone. 'During the drinking session he describes what happened with great pride'.

It appears that the event that the man described is not a rare or isolated event. The drivers who are just waiting, doing nothing, until a hire arrives are constantly on the lookout. It they see a boy who looks as if he is not familiar with the area, one of them will go up to him and get talking. After he finds out a little, another will casually speak to the boy and they are only interested in whether something can be obtained from him.

The driver who spoke to the girl referred to earlier realized that she had made arrangements to go back home several hours later. Having missed her appointment she was not sure what to do with her time. The man then suggests that a girl should not be alone and offers to drop her off at his home where she can spend time with his mother and sister and go back later. She is grateful for his protection and goes with him and finds that his mother and sister have gone out and she has to wait till they return. Few girls are as gullible as this, but the less gullible too can be seduced to part with something or the other that the clever 'confidence trickster' wants.

These stories are exchanged with pride, and everybody learns how to use opportunities. The behaviour of the man with the least scruples is made acceptable in the drinking milieu, and the others learn to follow the easier set of rules and don't feel that it is so bad do some things that they may have earlier felt was nasty. Taking all the money off a village boy who had come looking for someone regarding a job and leaving him helpless becomes acceptable through the subsequent bragging about it in the drinking session. Any bad feeling he may have had about the helplessness of his victim is converted to a feeling of pride when the others praise his cleverness. Soon he is able to say these things in the 'normal' setting to his crowd without having to wait for the drinking occasion.

3.8.4 Some contrasts

The average income of the three-wheeler drivers is probably double that of those in the cooperative shop described earlier, but their lives are much poorer. Just as with the village poor who had higher income than the cooperative shop staff here too the income is not the single biggest factor that determines the poverty of the people's lives.

The cooperative shop is therefore important for comparison. One feature we found there was that those with small incomes too had to conform to standards of the 'middle classes'. Another was that few members consumed alcohol (or tobacco or other drugs) daily. The third feature on which the shop differed was in giving people a monthly income instead of one daily.

Places of entertainment and leisure

3.9.1 Hotels

Our field assistant had to enter this setting as a customer and later get to know the staff. The process required about seven visits, and these could not be done on consecutive days, but at intervals. Initially the field assistant was a single customer, but with time he learnt how readily he was accepted into drinking circles. Where alcohol was not being consumed, he could not with equal readiness pull up his own chair and gradually become part of the group.

What are called 'hotels' are mostly places where people come to get food and drink. These are what would be called 'restaurants' elsewhere. Bigger hotels attract a different clientele from the smaller. In the smaller hotels people come and eat quickly and then leave. Some may linger a few minutes after the meal to have a cup of tea with or without an accompanying cigarette.

The bigger hotels are more 'classy'. These are not the upper end expensive hotels, but places where a group can sit around a table the whole evening eating and drinking. People come here to spend their time 'enjoying' rather than just to fulfil a need for food.

Richer regular customers have their own special table or tables. They are usually a group of middle aged men. They order their drinks first, usually a 'quality' arrack, and various 'bites' to go with it. They chat around a bottle of alcohol for over an hour and then order and have their food. The hotel staff know these customers, know their needs and routine and know how much of a 'tip' they will leave. They do not shout or make a lot of noise.

Not-so-rich groups too come to the hotel. These are usually a set of friends from the same workplace who want to enjoy themselves once a month or so. Unlike the regular, better-off customers these groups are very loud and conspicuous. They want attention, and want to demonstrate that they are having fun. They will order beer or arrack and are keen to show their drink to others. So they will stand up, walk up to another table as if looking for somebody, all the while holding their glass of alcohol high and visible and talking loudly from a distance to their friends still sitting at the table. Later in the evening they will walk with exaggerated unsteadiness and talk about being high.

Although they show that their usual inhibitions are not operative any more, they do not become violent or aggressive in this setting. This hotel is at a slightly higher status than their usual settings, and they somehow do not display the common tendency they have to become abusive after alcohol in other settings.

A group of six workers for example, working in a 'garment factory', all of them between 24 and 30, comes in at 7.00 p.m. or so. They too order 'bites', but not a lot of expensive ones (a sliced omelette rather than roasted meat). They have dinner and leave relatively early (work starts early the next day). Their conversation is stereotyped. Early in the evening the subject is people and incidents at the workplace and jokes about their bosses. Girls and women at the workplace are also

The association of 'fun', leisure and enjoyment is restricted to legal alcohol consumption. The same molecule - ethyl alcohol - in illicit alcohol cannot provide the same fun or enjoyment.

the subject. This is just to describe the attributes of different females. So there is merriment discussing the apparent ugliness of someone or vanity of another.

Later on the subject is usually sex. Each one describes some recent sexual incident and the details of the activity that took place, the reactions of the partner and so on. These conversations can be overheard by others, but not many are interested. Sexual activities with their regular girl friends are also discussed in this forum. Sometimes the girl friend is someone known to the others too, and the narrator takes delight in telling them how his girl behaves in bed, especially (it appears) because they too know her and see her everyday. Parts of her anatomy that they do not see are described along with how she responds sexually.

Some stories are about people and events in their home towns or villages. Even though the accounts appear rather fantastic, nobody is accused of making up and describing experiences that did not happen. The themes are nearly always sex, enjoying drinking occasions or getting into fights and assaults. The fighting is reported to be after alcohol, and they describe their own tendency to assault others when drunk. Remarkably none of them becomes aggressive in this setting.

By the time the meal is over all of the group are 'disinhibited' and jolly and loud. When the bill is brought, one person may loudly offer to pay it all. Someone else too then offers to share, but on all occasions the bill ends up being shared. Our field assistant too leaves with the group and gets more detail of their economic and other relevant particulars. Long conversations happen on the way back.

A later calculation shows that each person in the group gets a salary of about 4,000 to 5,500 rupees a month of which they spend about 2,500 to 3,500 on lodging and meals. This leaves each one about 1,000 to 2,000 or so 'spending money' per month for all needs, beyond day to day survival. They do send some money home to support their families too. Of the 1,000 to 2,000 that each person has available for a month, the evening's enjoyment usually costs about four to five hundred rupees.

The money is spent in a setting where more wealthy people 'enjoy', so the evening has some value beyond the alcohol and the food consumed. It gives them a subject to talk about with the friends who did not join in the evening's festivities, and it is not just a subject to talk about, it is also a way of showing who they are, or can be.

Hardly any families come in the evenings to these hotels and hardly any women. There are men who come alone too, to sit at a table and drink beer or arrack for about an hour and then leave after having dinner. These 'single' men do not look very wealthy either. Some of them come only on a weekend or holiday while there are others who come almost daily.

3.9.2 The shopping mall

Shopping malls are special in that they allow even the very poor to walk side by side with the very rich. They allow our research assistants too the same opportunity. After a time a 'culture' of the mall can be recognized. This is created by the regulars who linger. They don't all come every day or talk to every one of the other regulars, but they recognize and acknowledge each other. They know what happens in the mall.

Rich people come to the mall to buy things, to look at the shop windows and eat and drink. They do not realize that they are often being observed by another group, mostly poorer young men, who are studying their clothes, ornaments, style and behaviour. Some rich people come as a families or as mother and children. Some mothers like to come with their children dressed well and walk around to be seen. They may buy something they need or don't need.

Poorer folk too can come in, linger, look at windows and the food and drink, spend as much time as they wish and leave without spending any money. The poor get the opportunity to see what the rich do as well as to be physically near them, to see what they wear, how they talk and walk and the accessories they carry. The rich don't particularly notice the poor.

Celebrities too drop in. An athlete, sportsman or sportswoman or film star walk across and everybody points to them. Some are identified as sons of ministers or well known businessmen. Others with money come here as a convenient meeting place or rendezvous. Rich, young men come to the car park with their girls and stay inside with the engines running and air-conditioning on. The poorer youth who walk around see this too. They may walk into the car park as a part of their exploration or sightseeing.

A group of very attractive young men and women are regularly seen smoking. They sit and smoke in a way that displays their smoking as a sign of pride and to be displayed. Smoking inside the mall was previously not permitted, but these groups seem to have forcibly created 'spaces' where displays of smoking is now accepted. This group can be seen frequently with 'Western' women who also smoke or walk around with beer cans. They are lavish with their money. Our assistant claimed that even a newcomer can get food or drink at their expense, if they link up with them.

There were a few 'foreign' girls in very short skirts, with beer cans in one hand and very ostentatiously shown cigarettes in the other, who came and spent time regularly. Our field assistant says that they were dressed in a way that 'attention was all on them'. They always sat or stood on the ground floor in the area where they could be seen from all the upper floors too. Our field assistant says,

'They stood at this most prominent place almost on every day that I was doing the observations here. They come off and on, drink beer and smoke on occasion, talk loudly and draw attention to themselves – even though their skimpy clothes already do that enough. But they did not look as if they were looking for customers for sex. They always leave together in the same group'.

Some malls have become settings where people come to meet other people, or hope to meet other people. These probably include encounters for sexual intimacy too. Several young men and women are seen just 'hanging around'. They are on the lookout for others who may pay attention to them. When they do pay attention they may casually happen to get into a short conversation, and they can then be seen leaving together.

Some of these persons were quite open about why they were spending time at the mall. They were willing to share information about themselves with little reticence.

Example: Sudath

Sudath is 18, from a poor home. He comes to the mall after classes. He loves to look at new fashions, dancing and models. He is ready to go with a man who summons him for the evening, but only if he can get money. He goes also to the beach where he may meet a wealthier man who would like to take him away. He will not go with anybody who does not want to give him a gift. Other than this he is always looking out for girls who will go out with him, but spending time with girls costs money.

'If I get five hundred rupees that is enough for me to live for a day or two. My father gets a small salary and all that he earns goes for alcohol. Nobody is interested in what I do. I can sleep at home or at a friend's house, and I don't have to tell beforehand whether I will come home. If I don't go home in time, I will have no dinner, but dinner is not very grand anyway.'

Sudath and others like him want money to get the right clothes and other trimmings. This may be a particular wristband or cap. A handkerchief to tie around his forehead has to be of the type that is now used by others. If he meets a girl just to walk around with, he needs money. He gets ideas about what to wear from looking at 'Music TV', from film star magazines and by observing rich boys. All he likes to do is be with friends, walk around with them. The more friends he has the better. A gang of ten will be much better than just walking with two others.

Sudath and many others in the mall 'cut classes' and use the time to loiter in places like this. He is referring to tuition classes, which are held in the afternoons. They try to show younger boys in the class that they are having great fun outside and get them too to join. A younger boy may come with more money than what Sudath has. Then he is able to cover some of the day's expenses from that boy's money.

Example: Srima

Srima is about twenty-eight or so and has a young son whom she brings to school every morning. She drops in to the mall and spends time until 1.00 p.m., after which she has to take her son back home. Srima has great financial difficulties. One of the groups of rich young men who walk around the mall have met her before, and if they are there, they invite her to go out for a drive and then drop her back in time to pick up her son.

'I don't drink alcohol, only a beer. These friends get offended if I don't have even a beer when they are drinking it in the car. We go out to some interesting place and they drop me back and it is better than just killing time here.'

Srima is quite definite that people lose their inhibitions when they consume alcohol.

'Actually I don't like beer very much, but, you know, after a beer you really don't care where you are or what you are doing.'

Shopping malls are special in that they allow even the very poor to walk side by side with the very rich. Rich people do not realize that they are often being observed by another group, mostly poorer young men, who are studying their clothes, ornaments, style and behaviour.

3.9.3 Other leisure settings

Galle Face Green
This space of green facing the sea beach is used by many people to walk or to sit down on the grass and relax in the evenings. People come here to walk or jog for exercise in the mornings. They may come as a group or individually, but they do their exercise and leave. In the evenings it is quite a different matter. Many people come to spend their leisure here sitting around or promenading. Not many really wealthy people are seen spending their leisure here.

The green is a free space for anybody to enjoy without having to pay any money, so it is a poor man's leisure venue. We asked our field assistant to spend a few days in this setting for this reason. The shopping mall too is a setting in which someone can sit around without having to pay for the privilege, but it is not used by poor families, only poor youth. The green is used by poorer families too, to spend some time relaxing.

Poorer families, groups of not so well to do boys and couples come to Galle Face to spend the evening. Vendors of different kinds sell things to eat or drink and other trinkets. People generally sit in groups chatting to each other. In these groups they do what they have learnt to do for leisure.

Some years ago there were often fights and brawls too, because groups would consume alcohol and then become aggressive for the slightest provocation. A few months before our study commenced the authorities prohibited the consumption of alcohol on the green. Now groups could be seen who were consuming alcohol surreptitiously. They would bring their alcohol in 'soft-drink' bottles and pretend they were not consuming alcohol, but they would still probably consume the amounts that they were previously using. Now it is with little fanfare and display.

Groups could be observed leaving after a few hours of drinking alcohol together. There would be some members who were unsteady because of their relatively higher intake, but they try hard not to let it be visible because it was no longer a 'drinking' venue. They were not provoked to be aggressive or boisterous as they were previously when they were intoxicated. There is hardly any fighting and aggression on Galle Face Green even though people are still drinking alcohol as before.

'Walking' - pavements, junctions and crowded places
Young people with little money have to innovate leisure activities. Some of these youths that our field researchers met at the malls or at Galle Face Green, described what else they do for leisure. A common leisure activity was 'going walking' (*avidinna yanawa*). 'Going walking' in Sinhala means 'going out' too, but one form of going walking is in fact literally walking. These groups would walk along roads where there were shops and restaurants simply looking at whatever was going on, and looking for opportunities. Our field assistant joined in two of these walks for a few hours.

In such a walk they may stop at a junction and chat to each other, look at passers-by and see whether an opportunity existed to link up with someone interesting.

The Galle face green is a free space for anybody to enjoy without having to pay any money, so it is a poor man's leisure venue. This space of green facing the sea beach is used by many people to walk or to sit down on the grass and relax in the evenings.

They'd disperse in groups of two or three and meet together again as the larger group to walk on to the next 'spot'. In these places they will always be on the lookout for vulnerable persons who may be an easy target. It is a matter of skill as to what they can extract from each such individual 'victim'.

A small success will be to get free food using a person they just met. They'd invite a new-found friend to a restaurant and offer him snacks and tea, for instance. Then they'd pretend to want to go to the toilet and escape from the restaurant leaving the unsuspecting new friend to pay the bill for everybody. This kind of thing would be resorted to if the victim appeared not to have much money. Larger scale earnings are possible but rare. Trying to make friends with someone who will feel sorry and buy something for them is the commonest tactic. With longer-term contacts it is possible sometimes even to get a 'loan'.

When they do get some money through fair means or otherwise, it is spent mostly on clothes and other 'extras' to help them look like the rich young men. Imitation materials are available at low cost, to resemble what the rich youth have. If there is money left over, it is spent on eating and on drinking alcohol at more 'high class' settings. They too order 'lemon gin' and not arrack, and boast for weeks about the special effect they got with lemon gin, compared to arrack. People from their background haven't even heard about lemon gin and certainly can't afford to drink it at the places that these young men have visited.

The young men from the cooperative shop too bought lemon gin once a year and spoke about it for another year. Young and unemployed youths have discovered that the way of showing a really special experience is to spend money on lemon gin. The field assistants in the two settings were different and so neither was able to follow up on how 'lemon gin' had acquired this aura of class and sophistication among two widely different groups of poorer and less privileged young men living in the city.

The poorer youth encountered here seem to have worked out many different strategies to savour what they believe to be the pleasures that the city offers to those with money.

3.9.4 Role models and others of influence

Less affluent young men learn about rich youth drinking lemon gin and aspire to experience it even once. Rich or wealthy young men are the most important role models for the poorer youth. How the model behaves, is picked up by constantly studying them, following them and perhaps even talking to them, if the opportunity arises. This is not readily possible.

Those who have opportunities to associate with the rich youth provide the link. They come back and tell the others how the rich guys spend their time, what they wear, where they get their clothes, the accessories that are currently fashionable, the kinds of alcohol and other drugs that they use and what they do for sexual pleasure. Our field assistant felt that some of these stories may not come from any real fraternisation with richer youth, but from imaginary associations created for better status.

There are some among the less affluent groups too who are better informed about such matters than the rest. They too are influential because they know more about things than the others. They take careful note of hairstyles, clothes and other fashions from TV programmes and film magazines. There are less affluent young men who travel to India to bring thing to sell. These guys too are better informed about the styles and fashions in India and they wear something that is not freely available at present in the Sri Lankan shops. This makes them stand out. Most of this group are reported to be Muslim youths.

Perhaps the most influential within a group are the members who have a little more money than the rest. The other influential persons are those who know most about the subjects of interest – such as fashion, music, money-making and opportunities for sex.

Young men who work wearing a necktie are looked up to, whether they are rich or not. Only a certain category of office employee wears a necktie. A clerk does not wear a tie, so there is an implication of higher status of the man who wears a necktie, even though it is not strong proof that the person is rich. There are others who are not of the same status who too wear a tie, but they will not talk to each other in English. The ones who are to be copied are young, wear a necktie and speak to each other in English.

Poor lives in Colombo – final impressions

Lives of many people are poor in Colombo. They are poor in the range of things to do and be involved in, poor in variety of interests, poor in aspirations to aim for and poor in comfort and opportunities to enjoy leisure. The lives of women are remarkably poorer than that of men.

How do the lives of the economically least privileged compare with those of 'middle class'? We have no comparative data.

The middle class woman probably has a more comfortable physical environment in which to live. She will probably sleep on a more comfortable bed, for example, and hardly ever sleep on the floor. She will probably be less likely a victim of violence or aggressive behaviour by the husband (of this we have no strong data). But she too will work at a full time job outside the home, do all of the cooking and housework, and watch television as the main, or only, leisure activity. Among men, the difference between those of 'middle class' and those economically least privileged is probably higher. The middle class man is less likely to smoke, he will read a little more, and he will have less threat of involvement in physical violence or aggression. The lives of children will likely differ considerably between the 'middle class' and the least privileged. The most striking difference will be in their aspirations. Middle class children will dream of becoming an engineer, teacher, doctor, or lawyer. None of the informants in our study ever mentioned any such aspirations for their children. This is despite 'free education' for all.

3.10.1 Lives of the economically deprived in Colombo

What are the most striking things we have found about poverty and life in the urban setting?

Firstly that the term 'poor' hides a great deal of intra-group differences. The poor are of many levels.

Many of the most poor in the city are crowded together. Much of the character of their lives is derived from this one fact. They are unable to 'wall themselves off', for example as a family, from what happens in their community. The poor in the village and the not-so-poor in the city have a slightly better defined space, a boundary.

3.10.2 'Porosity'

Because of not having a boundary beyond which the rest of the world or community cannot intrude (or 'porosity' of the living space), the poor in the city will find it difficult to improve economically. A slight growth in income or wealth will be recognized., and demands made on the slightly better off, at times of hardship or crisis, will be greater.

The people who appear to be able to improve their physical circumstances, whilst still residing in the crowded community, appear to be those who somehow managed to wall-off or separate their compound physically. To build a wall or fence around your house in an overcrowded setting requires a good deal of power and a certain lack of concern for what other people may feel or say. To have a gate which can be shut or locked is quite unusual.

The 'porosity' affects even family and sex life. Privacy is difficult. At the same time there is, paradoxically, more opportunity for sexual liaisons outside of marriage. To 'jump the fence' when a moment's opportunity arises is part of common parlance. Poverty in the city goes hand in hand with becoming part of a crowd, even at home. Severe poverty entails a loss of physical boundaries for the self and the family.

3.10.3 'Jealousy'

Combined with a feeling of envy for anybody who rises above the rest, the forced sharing of all life and life circumstances is a further hindrance to any family moving up, economically. Whether this tendency, to want to keep all others no better than oneself, is a feature outside this kind of community has to be studied. But it certainly is a strong element in these communities. Many of our informants have referred to this as 'jealousy'.

Jealousy is most evident in relation to money and material possessions. So anybody getting some unexpected windfall will be forced to spend it all in celebration. This is a legitimate way of getting them to squander what they have got. After a time this becomes the norm or 'natural' thing to do with all extra income. We saw the same tendency reflected in the rural areas too.

Physical improvement in the household or appliances will similarly draw attention to the family, if the 'level' of these exceeds the norm. More subtle improvements are hindered too. A couple that is happy together will be envied. Once noticed there will be small attempts to undermine their joy. A man who does not consume alcohol daily with the crowd can be targeted in the same way. He can be asked to contribute to celebrations or events or some other community need and a measure of pressure can be applied to make him do so.

Alcohol was said to afford a unique opportunity for the 'jealous' to ensure that others don't surpass them. This is because alcohol use is associated with social interaction without inhibitions. People who are to be targeted can be readily singled out and harassed with no impediments at all. They can be pressed or persuaded, in the drinking setting, to comply with what the group wants. The most vociferous few strongly influence what the group as a whole wants. Compliance includes behaviour outside the drinking setting too. What someone did this morning can be brought up at the drinking session, and the person criticized, condemned or attacked. People can similarly be told how they should behave in their day to day lives, and their failure to comply can be brought up for comment at the next drinking session.

3.10.4 'Powerful individuals'

Another feature of the life of the poor in the city is the presence and influence of 'powerful' groups or individuals. Significant control is exerted by vested interest groups on how the poor live day to day. These influences are really a manifestation of powers outside the community. A 'big person' outside determines the limits of some things that people may do. How much freedom a visiting researcher may be given too is probably regulated by agents representing the 'authorities'.

This constitutes a major compromise of autonomy, but it is not felt as an imposition by people there. They have probably always learnt to keep within given limits. There are some people within the community whom others do not challenge. They do not intrude too much into people's private affairs but the fact that they can, if they want to, is felt.

Lack of control

The most striking factor of the way that the poor spend money is that they seem to be governed even more than the rich by how others think they should spend money. The poor spend money on things that will give them social credit. So do the rich, but the rich seem to have less direct pressure than the poor on how they should live. Others don't accost the rich man and abuse or criticize him if he does not conform. The rich man may like to impress his peers, but he is not subjugated by them. The poor man in the city is rather less free to do as he chooses.

If a poor family does not wish to have a party when their daughter reaches menarche, it will have to explain why it did not. A middle class family may decide not to have a party for this event. They may be criticized out of their hearing, but in a poor family the parents will be asked directly why they are not doing their duty by their daughter.

Others in the community will feel that they have a right to demand an explanation. They may even be able to reject and over-rule this explanation. Somebody else may come forward to hold the party! The same goes for funerals and weddings (other than secret weddings resorted to for some presumably embarrassing reason).

Impossibility of overcoming poverty

A comment that struck us was that people could not emerge from poverty as long as they lived in that setting, irrespective of the income they were able to earn. One factor underlying this is the 'porosity' of living arrangements that we referred to earlier. There is no room for slow growth or development out of sight of others, and others are not necessarily all happy to see one family prosper.

The factors underlying this include alcohol.

3.10.5 Alcohol and other substance use

The centrality of alcohol or heroin use for the majority of adult men is another visible feature in the most underprivileged settings. Tobacco too is consumed heavily. Everybody knows that the trade and use of illicit drugs and illicit alcohol is not to be challenged, beyond a certain point. Tobacco may be an equally pervasive and harmful influence on the lives of the poor in the village, but the freedom to criticize it, to challenge it and to try to reverse its grip on the community has not been taken away.

The effect of alcohol on the community is enormous. It is not just the money that is spent on alcohol., but that money too is considerable.

There are means by which the heavier drinkers make others pay for their alcohol. Forcing every occasion to be an 'alcohol occasion' is one of these. Then creating the feeling that much alcohol must be served for a 'proper' party or occasion is another.

People who are new to the group or junior have to take up more of the bill when they go out. Collecting money from light alcohol users and non-users too, when events or celebrations are organized, is common. In all of these, the cost for alcohol is not registered by either party as a alcohol expense, should someone try to compute the money spent on alcohol.

Newcomers to the city are made to contribute to the 'fun' and alcohol use of their seniors – urban and rural. There are experts at siphoning out money from the pockets of recent arrivals from the village. Some older hands manage to utilise their own earnings for themselves and their families whilst using the money of others to have 'fun'. Those who have to contribute most for this are rural young persons working on their first job in Colombo. More senior people in their workplace and boarding have perfected the art of withdrawing money from their pockets.

Behaviour in drinking settings

What the poor say and do in their drinking settings is very different from what the rich do. The behaviour that people learn to display in drinking settings spills over to the rest of life. In the drinking setting, poor people are allowed to transgress personal boundaries to any extent they wish. Those who want to control what others say and do are able in the drinking setting to tell them what they should do. They can also question anybody on whatever subject they choose.

No question is out of order. A stronger person in the drinking group can ask another anything he wishes, and the other is obliged to answer. The stronger person gets the right during the drinking event to comment and criticize the conduct of others in the community. He can also tell them how they should conduct themselves in future.

Striking differences are visible in the way that alcohol affects behaviour. A wealthier group consumes alcohol at the same hotel as group of poorer workers who have come there to drink as a special treat, but only the poorer drinkers become noisy and conspicuous. When alcohol is used surreptitiously in places where it is prohibited, people who have consumed enough to make them unsteady still do not become loud and aggressive – although they did when it was not prohibited and therefore openly consumed.

Other substance use

Alcohol and heroin are an integral part of the lives of many people in poor communities. Tobacco use is too, but it is somehow less noticed or commented upon. The total amount spent by the community on tobacco will probably not be that much less than what is spent on alcohol, but alcohol and heroin receive much more attention than tobacco does.

Alcohol, poverty and crime

Criminal acts and violence appeared rather close to the surface in the poorest communities. Whether similar degrees of violence and criminality in richer communities are somehow hidden is debatable. The overall impression is that violent and aggressive behaviour is always lurking somewhere behind the scenes, and it is as if this tendency influences and controls much of life in the poorest communities.

The impact of alcohol on public norms about morality was described and highlighted repeatedly. This issue is taken up in the general discussion later. The 'license' afforded by alcohol to say and do things without too much worry about the consequences has many impacts. It certainly assists the physically strong or aggressive to dominate others, and we learnt that alcohol was used as a means of keeping people within the community developing beyond the level of their neighbours.

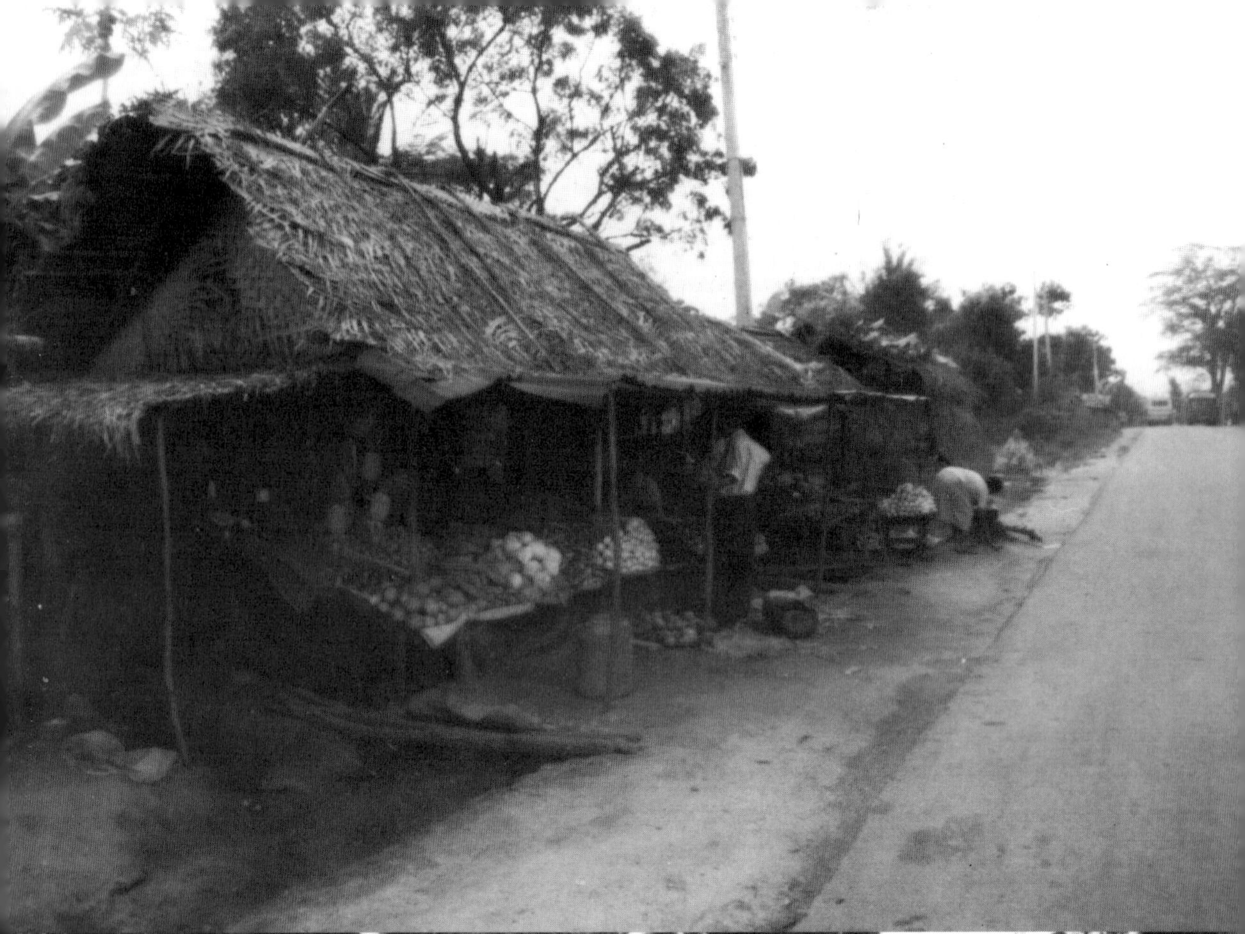

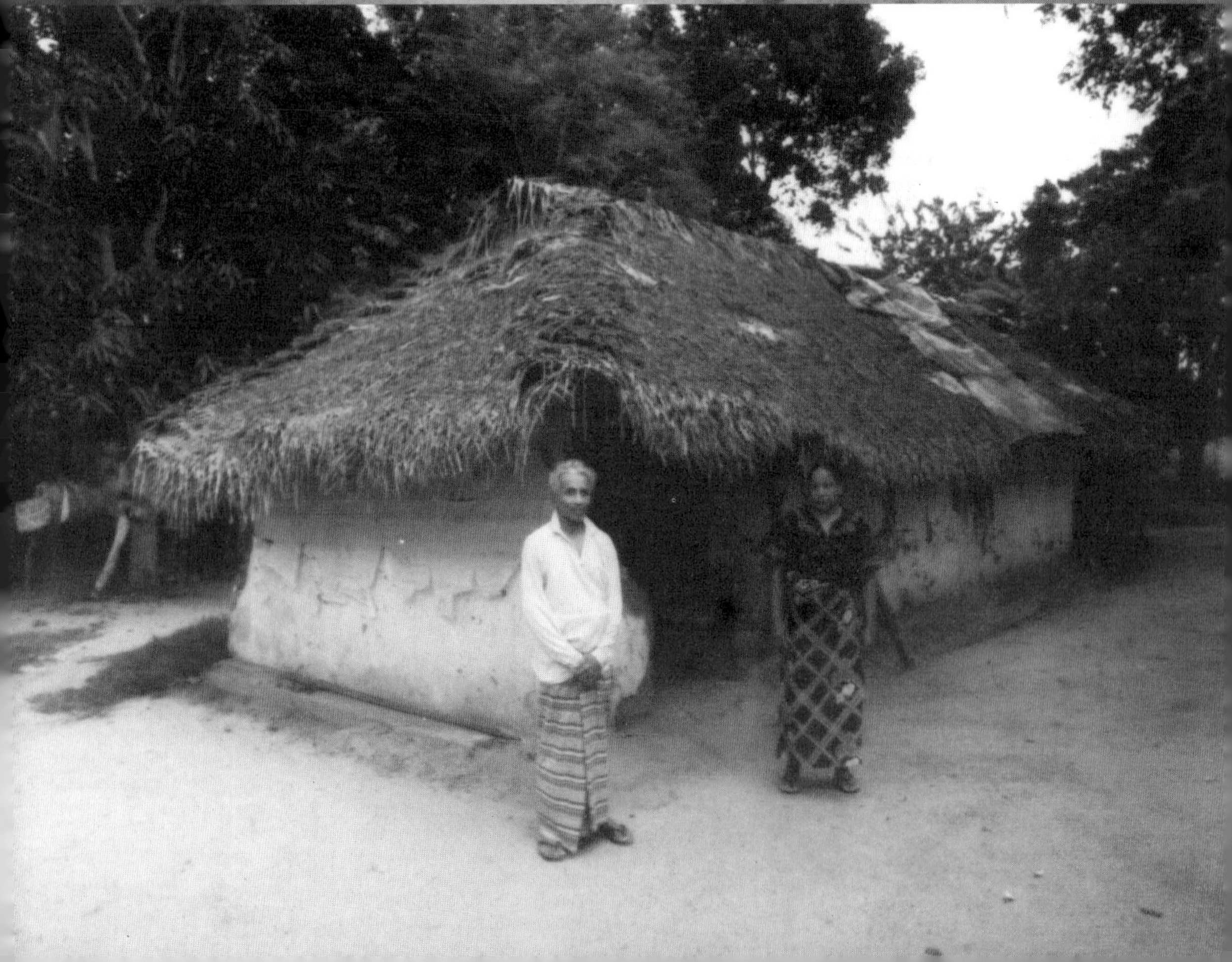

Rural Settings

Rural settings: poverty and alcohol use

This chapter starts out by describing the different rural settings that we have looked at. Each is next described. Since there is much in common between these settings regarding norms of consumption, alcohol use and consequences of its use these are summed up for all the settings at the end of this chapter.

Dry zone: poverty and vulnerability

4.1.1 The dry zone villages

Three villages in the dry zone were subject to ten days' field work each, one in Katharagama, Mihintale, and Polonnaruwa. In two of these villages the majority had settled there approximately 50 years ago. In all three villages most people are Buddhists.

In the village in Mihintale most villagers live on chena cultivation and this is an important income source in the Katharagama village too. Almost every family is engaged in paddy cultivation in the village in Polonnaruwa.

In all three villages the income sources are insecure, and the villagers are vulnerable to droughts. For instance in Katharagama we were told that the villagers face several difficulties in their farming. As they have one rainy and one dry season, whatever is planted in the rainy season gets destroyed during the drought. Usually there is no rain for six months. This means that they must survive through the dry season on what they have earned before this period.

In Katharagama, another income source for the villagers, probably even more insecure than the farming, is gem mining. A few informants describe this as the main income source. There are a few people who have earned well from this business and built their own homes. According to several informants, many mines are dug illegally, and are frequently raided by the police.

Another income source that is special to Katharagama, is from pilgrims. But even this is as uncertain and seasonal as others. Most visitors come to Katharagama during the weekend. During these days small businesses profit but during the rest of the week there is no such luck. Even during the festival season the income depends on the crowd. Some villagers make necklaces to sell, some help in the small sweet stalls, tea stalls and grocery shops and earn a living during this period. The pilgrims also bring food and different items that they distribute randomly among the villagers. The dry rations given can be enough for three to four days. Then people stay at home without going for work.

Income in the dry zone is irregular. But for many, the day's expenses have to be met by what is earned on the day.

In all the three dry zone villages, there are women working in garment factories. Some work as housemaids in the Middle East. We also heard that this creates problems and that many villagers are reluctant to go abroad. The trip is expensive, and villagers have to borrow money from various sources to go. Once abroad their earnings are sent to pay back the loans.

Of course the consequences of going abroad differs from woman to woman, and from family to family. Some have earned well but some are at the same state as before. Some have built their own homes and bought furniture and are now doing well. In some homes where the wife has gone abroad, the husband wastes the money on alcohol, we were told.

4.1.2 Poverty, indebtedness and gambling in the dry zone

Poverty is a common theme in all the informants' stories in the dry zone. We were told that it is difficult to find a family who had developed by saving money. As the income is small they cannot save. Sometimes poverty represents a vicious circle. Even if someone finds a position for a jobless person, he may not have the money for his travelling. What is earned in that day meets the day's expenses. Many families are Samurdhi-beneficiaries. But if the family has a bike or if a member in the family is abroad, they will not receive such support.

Loans and indebtedness seem to be an important part of everyday life. There are moneylenders in the villages, and loans are relatively easy to get. Some take loans for a wedding, planning to pay back from the money received as presents.

People also take loans from the Samurdhi or Community Development Society to finance their weddings, often claiming that the intention is some kind of income generation. We were told that for a wedding a person would take about 15,000 to 20,000 rupees as a loan. The housing loans people take are repaid monthly. They pay about 150 rupees per month. If they do not pay they know that they will have to go to court. Normally the loans are about 7,500 rupees. Some take loans to finance their court cases. According to one informant, a sum of about 2,000 to 3,000 rupees is spent for travelling and the lawyers' charges during one hearing.

Particularly in the Polonnaruwa village, the debt and loan or credit formed a kind of cycle. The villagers get an income from paddy cultivation twice a year, during the Yala and Maha season. When they do not cultivate they buy their needs from the stalls on a credit basis. If you take 20 families, 18 of them are in debt, we were told:

If they are in debt for 25 rupees last month, they pay only 10 rupees and keep the remaining 15 to the next.

The money earned from paddy is spent on items such as a television set or radio. During the times when paddy cultivation is not done and they are in financial crisis, they pawn these items or their paddy land to get money. When they get money they pay back and bring the items home. Again they pawn and this goes on like a cycle. Several of the informants complained that the majority of the villagers spend the money they earn on unnecessary things. *Even if they don't have a place to keep the paddy they buy a colour television from*

Income from paddy cultivation is seasonal. People then buy TV sets or radios. When there is no harvesting they are in a financial crisis and have to pawn these items, or their paddy land, to get money.

the harvest money, rather than building a room for the paddy. When it rains the paddy gets wet. They sometimes cover it with a water resistant cloth.

In Polonnaruwa the development of new technology has changed their way of cultivation What was done using cattle, is now done by tractors. They have to spend a large amount of money for the maintenance of these vehicles. Apart from this, fertilizer and other agro-chemicals also cost a lot. All this adds up to their difficulty in matching the expenditure with their earnings.

As mentioned above, a funeral is an occasion for spending. It is also an occasion for gambling, which seems to be a main feature in funerals in the villages. People from outside the villages also come to gamble.

To sum up, the economical situation of the dry zone villages is a situation of economic uncertainty, lack of steady income and poverty. In addition to the unquestionable objective poverty, there is also a certain element of what we could call subjective poverty, which seems to be an important hindrance to development. It also seemed that these villagers feel helpless. When poverty is regarded as destiny, or predetermined, it is seen as something to adjust to and live with rather than as something to fight.

Wet zone, closer to Colombo

We describe the wet zone community separately because we expected it to be less vulnerable and less desperate. We chose a village in Awissawella as our case community. As the discussion will show, the situation is very similar to what we experienced in the dry zone villages.

4.2.1 The wet zone village

The road to the village is bordered by rocks and a valley with a waterway. The coconut and rubber estates along with the virgin forests provide a continuity broken by the regular positioning of houses and the haphazard arrangements of large chicken farms. Lush greenery is constant throughout the village. Large areas of rubber estate are equally prominent, and from the time of daybreak both males and females are working in the rubber estates, transporting the extract produced or helping transport the processed sheets.

Most of the older generation of villagers have not attended school and cannot read or write. Among the newer generation very few have attempted the GCE O/L or A/L examinations. Even those who have attended grades 5 or 6 surprisingly cannot read or write even at a basic level.

The life style of the villagers follows a somewhat set and repetitive pattern. There is hardly any difference whether it is a weekday or weekend as there are no government sector or private commercial sector employees. Most being daily paid employees they seem to go to work when work is available and stay at home when there is no work.

Most people are daily paid. They can be seen working from daybreak, amidst the lush greenery of the rubber estate.

4.2.2 Poverty and economy in the wet zone village

The main income appears to be employment in the rubber estates. The daily wage is Rs.85/= for females and Rs.100/= for males. The other sources of income are all outside the village: working in river beds digging out sand, working in a wood factory, a quarry, as a daily paid labourer or, in the case of a few, in the armed forces. A relatively new and quite prominent income source is the poultry industry. An outside firm provides the hatchlings, the necessary food and medicine while the villagers have to make the cages and provide security. At maturity the firm pays the villagers an amount according to the weight of the chicken.

Here as in the dry zone, a number of women have gone abroad to the Middle East to work as housemaids. At the beginning there seems to be some return with the presence of a few items of electronic equipment. Often these are sold off in a few months after return in search of the elusive air fare cost and the cycle repeats itself.

Three outsiders come to the village to ply their trade. The fish monger on the bicycle, the sweep ticket seller cum ice-cream seller on the motorbike and the sweep seller on the push bike. Sweep tickets are a great and very significant drain of the finances of this village.

A fishing community

Our knowledge of the fishing community is based on observations and interviews in a village in Gampaha District.

4.3.1 The fishing village in Gampaha

Our field assistant described the place as "village where small motorboat and sailboat fishermen live". The sea borders the village on three sides, and the village was situated below sea level. Compared to the agricultural villages this was rather big, with 800 – 1000 households, living in tight quarters with 2-3 families in each house. The houses are situated very close to each other. Most of the villagers are illegally living in this land[1].

Even before entering the village a disgusting foul smell of rotten fish creeps in, and the smell intensifies as you get closer to the village. The wind, which brings this smell to the village, comes from the beach where parts of fish and droppings of crows and other birds rot. The village lacks trees and greenery.

Around five to six children live in each house. The small children did not look too healthy. Children from the age of 10 years help in the fishing industry. They collect fish from the fishermen and try to sell them. Some children play on the beach, because they do not have a garden at home or there is no room near their house. The majority of the elders were not educated. Even the youths were not well educated. The numbers attending school were few. They do not go for outside jobs as they earn well from their fishing business[2].

There is no difference in the daily routine whether it is a weekday or a weekend. They work if work is available or otherwise stay at home.

The coast around the village docks more than 100 motorboats and about 20 sailboats. Near each boat at least three to four people were seen working. They were preparing the fishing nets for the next trip. Some were seen in water, up to their waist, throwing fishing nets into the sea. This was one way of catching fish for the people who did not have boats. All the men our field assistant met were occupied with some work involving the fishing industry.

The houses have 2 to 3 rooms. They lack a kitchen or toilet. They use public toilets, which are maintained by the Town Council (TC). There are eight such toilets and the TC cleans it every two weeks. The five public taps along the road are rather dirty. People take water to drink, wash and bathe from these taps.

Depending on what they do as a living, the time their day starts varies. Men who go to sea start around 4 in the afternoon and end their day around 3 to 4 in the early morning of the next day. Some go out in the morning. When they return, they send messages to their friends to come to the beach. This is when these people's day starts. From 4 am till about 7am they cut the fresh fish to make dry fish. From 7am onwards the traders join in and selling of the newly brought fish takes place. The men who do not have boats throw their nets to the sea around 7am and end the task by around 11am. Generally all the work of the fishermen who go out to sea is over by 12 noon. The fish sellers are left to finish their trading and by 2 or 3 everybody leaves for home.

4.3.2 Poverty and economy in the fishing community

The economy of the village is closely connected to the fishing, and it also includes the women and the children[3]. Numerous employment opportunities are generated from the sea. Boat owners give income opportunities not only to the fishermen but also to people engaged in maintenance of the boats. At the next level are the 'mudalalis' or traders, the middle men and their helpers. Then there are ice/salt sellers, producers and sellers of fish baskets, fish sellers, people who cut the fish, and people who dry the fish.

The major problem to the whole village is the time of year when people cannot go to sea. During these months their economy drifts and the boat owners and fishermen leave for other villages. This causes loss of employment to a large number of individuals who depend on these boats and fishermen. They know however that after these months they will have work again. If they have saved at least something, it is used during this season or they pawn their jewellery or take loans. All this is for 2 to 3 months. When they start to earn again they pay back the loans and live their normal life.

To our field assistant the village seemed an ideal place for money generation. Anyone coming to the village can find various ways to earn from the fishing industry. Not all that is earned stays in the village. The field assistant saw many reasons for this:

The beach has parts of fish and droppings of crows, which creates a foul smell. The wind, which comes from the sea, brings this smell into the village.

Alcohol and Poverty

For them, money is not so valuable. If they can do something with 100 rupees, they would spend 150 without hesitation. Maybe this is because they earn from the sea, which they feel is a free source of income. The money carries no weight. Even the fishermen feel that what they earn is 'easy money'. After spending the night or a few hours in the sea, they spend whatever money they have earned on fuel, fishing equipment and the boat. The remaining is used to 'remove their tiredness'. 'We went to sea' is their slogan and they use it as a cover to spend their money to relax and enjoy the rest of the day. They are not afraid to spend. They know that they can earn more the following day.

One informant described the situation like this:
"There is no limit for a fisherman. A family has many children, but they get plenty to eat. As opposed to a government officer or a labourer, these men get benefits from nature. He comes, eats, drinks, nobody looks for faults. Today we eat, today we live and tomorrow we die, who cares!"

Because the villagers know that they can earn tomorrow again by going to sea, they are not afraid even to take large loans[4].

Men go to sea in the afternoon and return early morning. Then others come to the beach. This is when these people's day starts.

The estate community

Our conclusions about the estate community are based on field work in a tea estate in Kandy district.

4.4.1 The tea estate

The estate extends over 300 acres and belongs to the state. The tea factory was established in 1934 but is now closed. On the main road leading to the estate there are no shops but there is a bar. The bar seemed to be quite busy attracting not only the estate labourers but also the estate officers, police personnel and travellers and passers by, even in the morning.

The people are on average small built and are very lean. They are also very old looking when compared to the real age that they give. The literacy rate is quite low even though the exact figures are unknown[5].

There are 120 families on the estate, and of these around 80 families have employment on the estate. Out of these there are about 15 Sinhalese families. The main income comes from the tea estate, where the women gather tea leaves and the men do work like cutting the overgrown trees and spreading fertilizers etc. A typical working day starts around 7.00 am. The men finish their work by 2.00 pm but the women finish their work only at 5.00 pm. After work they carry the plucked tea down to a place where it is weighed and noted. Each person has a set amount of kilos that they have to pluck every day. The working conditions are difficult, and they have to brave the sun and the rain.

The women in particular are in a difficult situation; their day starts around 4.00 am cooking, getting the children ready for school and then going to work. When they return they have to make dinner and the cycle goes on[6].

In addition to the gulf between those working at the village and those working elsewhere, there is also a strong segregation and categorizations based on the work one does. These are also related to the caste system with jobs being associated with low and high classes. This caste system is deep rooted. The person one talks to, the one whose house can be entered, the one who can be entertained and the one to entertain, are all influenced by the system.

There are basically two types of houses on the estate. The individual houses are on the right hand side of the main road from the town, and the 'line houses' on the left hand side of the road. The line houses are a strong illustration of what we have called the porosity of the life of poor people, and they get their name from the way they are built. There are about fifteen to ten houses built together (as a row or line), each with a single room. The houses are separated from each other by the others' wall.

There are another fifteen houses on the opposite side. These are individual houses with a front garden and with at least two rooms. They are built quite close to each other and are separated by fences that only indicate the boundaries. One informant from this part of the estate gave an illustration of the porosity of the life in the line houses, when he said:

The women start the day at around 4.00 am; cooking, getting the children ready for school and then getting to work.

'Now when we come home after work we can stay home. Earlier, when we were in the line houses, there would be a lot of noise from men drinking, and the radios would be screaming through the night'.

The facilities on the estate are meagre. The most pressing problem apart from poor wages, as seen by the villagers, is the problem of water. It is immensely difficult during dry seasons to get water, and they say it affects their life.

There is access to electricity though not all houses have the facility. Around half of the households have a radio or television. But this is more scarce in the line houses. There are virtually no toilet facilities in the line houses. They share a very few poorly maintained common toilets.

4.4.2 Poverty and economy among the estate workers

Due to economic reasons the estate has seen a decline in people working there. Especially the younger generation is seeking employment outside the estate. They consider working on the estate degrading. However, the main source of income is still the tea estate. A person who works in the estate on average earns about Rs.120.00 per day and their monthly income is around Rs.1500.00. It should be more, but they say that the estate cuts their salary for EPF[7] and union fees. There are few other income opportunities within the estate itself. Some people used to rear cows, but this too has declined due to the fact that people regard the trouble as not worthwhile.

Some people from the estate have gone in search of jobs in the cities and some have even gone abroad. A person who goes to town to do daily manual labour, gets around Rs. 200 to 300 for a day. Even if he spends 50 for lunch and other expenses, he could still bring home around 200 and he could return home early too. Some women are also working in the garment factories. They apparently earn less than on the estate (Rs. 86), but consider that job as more honourable[8].

Shops commonly give credit, and as people buy on credit the shop owners also add a percentage to the retail price. As it is very difficult for these people to repay the debts, credit is regarded as a risky business for the shop owners. The shop owners normally have as collateral the EPF money, and they do trust that their dues will be settled because everyone knows everyone else in the estate. When the workers do get paid at the end of the month, they usually do not settle the entire amount they owe the shop owners. There is always some carry over to the next month.

The field assistant felt that one of the main reasons for their poverty is the lack of or rather absence of planning for the future. When the loan amount keeps increasing they respond to the owner of the shop when he brings up the issue by saying that they will never run away, and that they will at least pay it off using the EPF.

Another reason for their poverty could simply be that, because their resources are so limited and their income always less than their expenditure by a large amount, they have simply given up and take each day as it comes. Doing otherwise may only lead to greater despair and unhappiness. They also have to look after their elderly parents in most cases as these people lose their houses when they "retire" from the estate.

Communities of displaced persons, humanitarian crisis

We have data from two rather different communities of displaced persons, one in Puttalam and one in Vavuniya. However they have some important characteristics in common. Both communities are extremely poor, in every sense of the word. There is a great lack of not only financial capital, but also of social capital. And both communities represented a real challenge and several hardships to the field assistants visiting them. One indicator of the situation that complicated the interview situations was that any conversation with an outsider was quickly taken over with evident practice in showing and explaining their needs and requirements by virtually one and all. *"As you are from an organisation; well we don't have this and this ....; you could do this and this............but if that is too difficult, you could try this and this......"* According to the field assistant they go on and on in what would be comical if not for the desperate nature of their requests.

Both villages were rather depressing places to stay. We will start by describing the village in Vavuniya, and then come to the Puttalam village. The latter will be described in more detail than the other because of the particular situation in that village.

4.5.1 The village in Vavuniya[9]

The small, exclusively Tamil village is situated in the so-called "cleared areas" but with the LTTE having an unofficial say in the village. The village which is around 60 years old and comprises around 450 families, has around 300 families who have settled in after 1999.

The majority of the basic needs of these villagers have not been met. The people are seen to struggle to cope with their needs of housing, water, transport, electricity, health, and sanitary facilities. The new settlers are crowded into a relatively small area of around 2 – 3 acres centred around the school, cooperative shop and other shops. The land on which they now live belongs to the Government and they stay there technically illegally. The natives live some distance away with their houses spread out over a larger amount of land.

There is no electricity and the homes are dimly lit with the help of bottle lamps. The village has around five public wells constructed by UNHCR. These wells and a few more in the houses of the natives provide drinking water to the villagers. Water is scarce in the wells during the dry season. The sanitary conditions are not good. Five toilets built by UNHCR for the settlers are now crammed and emanate a terrible stench around the area. No functioning health care centre is currently present in the vicinity. Deliveries are conducted at home.

Many of the displaced persons have spent years in the refugee camps (welfare centres) before being relocated. This experience has of course affected them in several ways, not least the welfare of their children. One of the teachers at the local school commented that teaching the children from the camps was like trying to split a rock and make rope out of it.

The literacy rate is poor. Most adults seems not to be able to read or write.

There is barely any reading matter and no newspapers in the village. The school attendance is rather low. The school principal told that due to the relocation of the displaced, the school had got several new buildings along with other facilities, but out of around 300 students registered at the school 100 – 130 are absent daily.

The principal also said that most of the children lack birth certificates. Most marriages are unregistered and the couples have no marriage certificates. People do not even have National Identity Cards. What is important to them and what they carry about is the Temporary Identity Card provided by the army.

There are several small grocery shops located near the school and bus stop. There is also a cooperative shop where the Government rations are handed out. On the day close to Deepavali (Hindu festival) when this was done, our field assistant was present. He observed that many if not all the natives also obtained dry rations on the pretext of being displaced.

The natives' houses are two-roomed and fenced off from each other by means of thatched coconut palm leaves. The residences of the settlers are crowded together. There is no fencing between the houses and the houses are not really separated from each other. They are made of clay and the roofs made of thatched palms. There is no flooring. The houses are so low that one has to bend to enter. They are small, usually made up of a single room. There are usually no windows with a wooden board in the role of a removable door.

Our field assistant felt that that the natives and the settlers treated each other with mutual respect. Abeysekera (2002:126) however, describes that the native villagers have been opposed to the displaced settlers bathing in the village tank, refuse to accept their food offerings at the village temple, and oppose their using the village burial ground.

4.5.2 Poverty and economy among the displaced in Vavuniya

The poverty of the displaced community is illustrated by the state of their dwellings, the lack of furniture in them, their inadequate clothing, the state of their children and lack of even agricultural equipment. The life of the villagers depends heavily on agriculture. The main crop is paddy but it is cultivated only once a year due to water shortage. The native villagers own most of the land in the village, including all of the cultivatable areas. The settlers on the other hand do not own any land and are the labourers who work in the fields of the natives and of the neighbouring villages.

Some males have taken up hunting. Every day they bring hunted animals to the village to sell. Even people from other places come here to buy meat. Some meat is said to be processed and sent abroad.

The settlers depend significantly on the relief rations of rice, sugar and dhal, worth 1000 rupees, provided by the Government. It is worth mentioning that almost all the natives were also reported to obtain the ration presumably after obtaining signatures from the Grama Sevaka or

The community has not actually chosen this place to live, but has been driven there by circumstances.

headman of the village. The village as a whole has also benefited from other governmental and non-governmental agencies.

Kasippu brewing and selling play a crucial role in the earning as well as spending of this population. It seems that this is one of the main kasippu manufacturing places in Vavuniya. Many kasippu bottles are distributed to other areas from here. There are several reasons for this. One side of the village is bordered by the jungle and lakes, and this side is regarded no man's land, where neither the LTTE nor the government forces take much interest. Also the authority of other parts of the area remains undefined, so that no party is concerned with the illicit alcohol production, and nobody takes any action.

4.5.3 A village of displaced persons in Puttalam

Because of its extreme situation, we have chosen to give relatively more space to this village. It seems that among "our" communities, these people are really what is commonly called the poorest of the poor. The community has actually not chosen this place but has been driven by circumstances.

The community under study is a resettlement (or rather relocation) village not far from Puttalam on the west coast. It consists of around 400 families crowded together in an open expanse of dry sandy land. The resettlement area has been in official existence for the last 5-7 years though the initial displacement from their native lands in the North and East of Sri Lanka occurred twelve years ago.

Our field assistant stated that the community seemed artificial as if it was part of a "lego game". Large proportions have been settled in at once probably arranged by outsiders similar to a housing scheme or a block of apartments but in a much more disparate fashion. The houses are nearly identical, constructed from very poor concrete blocks, have very weak foundations, and occasionally just fall apart in the rain.

The part of the village that one encounters first has the appearance of temporary dwellings and looks like a refugee camp. Even though the settlers have lived in this location for the last 10 years, the cottages do not convey this impression. Why this is so, is a matter of great curiosity not only to the outsider but to the residents as well. One informant expressed that the residents here have enough money but don't like to show it, because then want help from donors who come to the area. One of the settlers living in this part of the village mentioned that the Government Agent of the district had *"identified our camp as the poorest one"*.

One part of the village is more pleasant, with tiled roofs on most houses. And the houses themselves are in a better state. The reason is that the around 40 families living here are being materially helped by a lady from Colombo. She collects money, clothes and even building material on their behalf.

The whole area is literally strewn with litter. There is no organized place or method to dump garbage, and this results in diverse methods being employed by the villagers. Most people dispose of waste by dumping it in the empty plots of land, while a few bury or burn the garbage. The garbage is mixed and as it is a windy open plain it is blown all over the area with especially the paper and the polythene bags being caught in barbed wires and other fences.

There is no community centre as such where there can be community interaction but there are three children's nurseries catering to about 20 children each. The state of children, especially the younger preschool ones, is very poor. Usually they have no clothes at all and are very dirty, with runny noses, thin but not emaciated, defecating in the lawns and playing about in this state out on the streets. Quite a large number of school-going children and certainly more than what could be expected can be observed not attending school. When their parents are questioned as to the reason the usual and common reply is that they are sick. Education is just not seen as something which is a means of escape but rather as a burden. This is illustrated by the friction produced when the school requests even the payment of the Rs.35 charged as facilities fees. This is the only payment to school for the whole term.

4.5.4 Poverty and economy among the displaced in Puttalam

The traditional employment for the majority was tailoring and business before displacement. In addition to the language issue and the obvious difficulty of starting a tailor shop anew they complain of an inadequate demand in the area and an already saturated market. For businessmen of course the greatest difficulties have been the complete loss of capital and the loss of contacts, both buyers and sellers.

More than 12 years since displacement several families still depend and live entirely off the dry ration. When the government is not able to provide the ration regularly, it is a big issue and one that causes great distress to them.

The efforts of the charity lady from Colombo have not made the settlers any less dependent or more innovative in finding solutions to their problems.

"Mrs Feroze (as we shall call the lady) said that she will come and build a wall around that well, but she hasn't come yet" says the male who is bathing from the well.

"Mrs Feroze said that she will find some money and build a religious school this year, but she hasn't turned up" says a former community leader.

"This road becomes all flooded when it rains. I told Mrs Feroze to repair it. God only knows why she hasn't come yet", says the elderly lady.

Our field assistant found that poverty was pervasive and striking in the area. No-one who is financially capable of finding another place would live here by choice. In effect poverty is what keeps them here.

The causes and maintaining factors of their poverty are complex. It could obviously be stated that the root cause of poverty for these people is their displacement from their homes in the north and east. But we have to remember that even before displacement, the vast majority of these people were poor back home as well. It was also found that those who are at least relatively well off amongst them are those who were financially better off back home. This is interesting considering that at the moment of displacement all were virtually at the same level, as if life was started all over again. One would have thought that the absence of any firm government or private sector jobs amongst the residents would have led to a more equal playing field. But it appears that the skills learnt earlier in life, or the lack of them in the case of most, seem to have made a difference.

The main 'industries', which drive the economy, are the scrap metals business, the 'vadai' (or fried snack) selling and a combination of tailoring, welding and other small businesses. The scrap metal business was started by some residents who collect scrap metal for weeks from far off places, transport the metal back to town and finally send it to Colombo for sale.

The "vadai" industry involves the making of a hot 'Maldive fish' dish, which is sold principally near bars. The youth, many of whom are involved in this, take their trolleys in which they make and sell the food item to many parts of the island – ranging from Colombo, Jaela, Puttalam, Anuradhapura and Jaffna. They claim they are the pioneers of this fairly innovative and commercially successful idea.

There are several factors which contribute to the problems faced by the community that are not noticed by the residents. Of the many traders coming to the village to sell their products throughout the day, there is not one who is from this resettlement area. The community depends on outsiders even for its basic needs such as thatched palms and poles for the cottages.

The practice of "seettu" is very rampant: a group of people get together and agree on the monthly amount payable per person, then draw lots to select the order of receiving the cash and collect a lump sum when their turn comes. In addition the residents are very prone to borrowing money from anywhere and everywhere. They borrow with interest from several grocery shop owners and other individuals within the community. There are others both at the nearest town and at Puttalam who lend larger amounts after retaining a security such as the land deed.

The villagers seem to have accepted the displacement, and if any bitterness exists it is not visible on the surface. They seem to have acknowledged that things could have been much worse as they could have been killed or physically harmed.

The views on the resettlement area in the nearest town are worth mentioning. Those outside the resettlement camp appear rather unsympathetic. A bank clerk stated that 'those people' are waiting for others to come and help them and are not capable of helping themselves. He felt that they will always like to live with the tag of the internally displaced as life is easier that way.

Villagers in Kataragama rely on pilgrims for their income. Stalls such as this which sell fruits for offerings at the Devale is thier main source of income.

Conspicuous consumption, envy and jealousy

Those that we met from rural settings handle their poverty in different ways. Their poverty clearly is not only a question of income. We have to bear in mind that most of the inhabitants of our villages are born poor, they are raised poor and they are socialised into poverty. It is no surprise that they may feel inferior, as one informant put it. Poverty seems to be regarded as a destiny. It is perhaps no surprise then that they react with apathy, which some of our informants confuse with laziness.

One way of handling the situation, of asserting one's character and confirming one's identity, is through consumption. This is best achieved through consumption that is visible to others. Extravagant weddings with lots of alcohol, wearing jewellery, or simply returning from town in a three-wheeler instead of walking, are all examples of this kind of visible consumption. In keeping with Thorstein Veblen's description of America more than 100 years ago, we could call this conspicuous consumption (Veblen 1953). It is a way of holding oneself to one's standards, and at the same time becoming the focus of the jealousy and envy of others.

What the villagers seek as indicators of success become, ironically, hindrances to development. In all the social settings we studied the way of spending was one obstacle to development. Another was envy and jealousy leading to active obstruction of people's development. Thus the very display of things intended to show progress serve to hinder progress. In the dry zone settings especially this is combined with a strong and rather condemning moralism. We also saw that the need for having a funeral or a wedding that is just as splendid or maybe better than the last one, is a cause of loans and indebtedness. One informant described how people in the village are fond of copying from each other:

They do not try to do what is best for them, but what is best to show off. Sometimes they fall in debt trying to do things this way. Finally they regret the way they have behaved. There are instances where people sold their land to finance weddings and even funerals. "What the neighbours do we must also do. Otherwise people will scold us and the children will be disappointed – so we have to do it this way" is how they think. Finally they even lose the place they live.

Similar stories were told in nearly all our social settings. The villagers seem to believe that spending shows that you are developed or rich. Therefore they work hard and earn money and buy a cassette player or something else that is a little expensive. This sort of spending is an important and visible aspect of village life. Therefore they spend their earnings on things, which they use to show others that they are rich. One informant in Mihintale said:

"For the funeral at our place we only got 7,000. The coffin alone cost us 7,500 rupees. Then the expenditure is too heavy for us. Anyway we had to spend about 25,000. Otherwise it is no use. If we buy a cheap coffin, people will scold us. They will ask 'What is this box?' If the funeral is done nicely, everybody will appreciate it"

One type of visible consumption is spending lavishly for festivals and celebrations. One informant among our tea estate workers told us that he had spent close to Rs 45,000 to celebrate the 'age attainment' or menarche of his only daughter. He justified the spending of such an enormous amount of money (compared to their daily wages) by the fact that she also suffers from asthma and may not live long.

Several informants looked upon this show-off tendency as a consequence of and a reason for poverty. It seems that particularly those who have been abroad, earning an income in the Middle East, are an easy target for envy and jealousy. We were told that women who went abroad are easy to recognize. They wear fancy clothes and lipstick, their nails are coloured, hair cut short and they wear too many gold chains:

When you see what these people bring back, others get excited and try to go abroad "If we stay here, we will never be able to buy those things, but if we go abroad, we'll be able to" is what they say. There are women who went to be able to build a house, but when they came back, there was no progress.

Also other informants told that the villagers are jealous about people who go abroad. We heard several stories of how people who had been abroad also liked to spend their money on unnecessary things, and how they hired a van to go to a good town and buy provisions for their homes. We also heard that women who had been housemaids in the Middle East were looked at with suspicion:

People who look at these women in a sarcastic way say: "How can they earn so much just by working in a house? They must be going out and getting involved in unwanted business." Men make these remarks generally, but sometimes women also join in.

It seems however that it is not only those who have been abroad who are envied, but everyone who is successful in one way or another. The statements below are from different informants:

"Some people are lucky enough to get continuous work at the same place. These are the people who become targets of jealousy from the not so fortunate".

"Some are jealous about others' progress. If one gets a donation or gift for something, it is not warmly welcomed. 'I didn't get anything, we also need something' is what they would say".

"If one leads a decent life by earning in a decent way, there are about 25 % to 30 % of people who look forward to seeing them fail".

"Most of the time people who have their own houses and their own vehicles become targets of individuals who have almost nothing. These people are so much involved in making traps for others that they lose what they have. These are the people who are useless not only to the village, but also to themselves and in the end lose what they might have".

In the fishing community there were various types of houses. While talking to the villagers our field assistant realized that people living in palm leaf thatched houses do not like the others to improve and build brick houses:

The people living in brick houses do not like others to come to their standard. Because of this, people living in houses of a lesser standard try to spend money to show that they are superior or equal to the so-called rich individuals.

Also in the fishing community visible or conspicuous consumption was a way of achieving prestige and status[10]. The field assistant noted that people seemed to give credit for lavish spending but the few villagers who have ignored this 'norm' have been able to establish themselves and now live well. He also noticed that a person who owns a boat would build a small house and buy various electrical items. There is often no space in the house to keep all the items. But it still demonstrates that they are similar to a businessman or that they belong to a particular class of the society.

As we noted earlier, this kind of consumption not only gives status – it is also a cause of envy and jealousy. One informant, a young unemployed woman living with her mother in the fishing village, told us:
"When we live well people are jealous. If we dress well, eat well and live happily others don't like it."

Whether people kept emphasising that others were jealous because they wanted them to be jealous is worth considering. Others' jealousy would be an affirmation that the person concerned had reached a level that justified jealousy.

Our field assistant felt that the 'norms' in this area have a great effect on the way money is spent. There are many complex cultures in the village. He felt that people are competing with each other and try to do better than the other.

Alcohol consumption as a part of everyday life

The most common form of alcohol used in all the villages studied is the illicit brew, kasippu. As legal arrack costs more, many drink kasippu. This, and the fact that kasippu is easily available, are given as the reason for kasippu use.

There were rather different ideas among our informants about whether the police cared about the illicit alcohol trade. Some said that the sellers get a good income and that even though they may have trouble from the police, not once have they been raided. Others told us that the 'kasippu joints' are raided buy the police once in a while and that the penalty is about 3,000 to 5,000 rupees. Some informants believed that the police do not want to interfere with this business. 'On the contrary, the police help these people'. The police raid the kasippu outlets but they do not take everything they find.

We were also told that kasippu is put in empty milk packets:

When we find them along the road we know what they are. One can find about 10 to 15 such packets in one day. On some days they stop selling because they are afraid that the police might arrive. Seven to eight people go off to drink during one day. They go independently and return quickly afraid of being noticed by others.

In Avissawella village the use of alcohol is rampant. Most of the alcohol consumed is illicit alcohol, kasippu. There are three to four places in the village which act as unofficial bars and stores. These are not apparent on first entry to the village as they are essentially normal looking houses. There is no place of licensed alcohol sale in the village or in the vicinity of the village.

The forest areas all around the village are reputed amongst the villagers to be hot spots for illicit brewing and selling of alcohol. The known houses which sell kasippu obtain the spirits in a nearby village from a large scale kasippu merchant. Kasippu is poured from gallons into glasses with ½ a bottle costing around Rs.20/=.

Most of the kasippu is served at evening or night though the sales places are open through the day. Those who work outside the village in sand quarries or in timber mills invariably after getting off from the bus proceed to one of these places and consume alcohol. While a minimum of ½ a bottle is consumed, in most cases it is much more. There are those who are said to consume kasippu throughout the day.

The owners of the kassippu stalls are villagers who used to be, or are still employed as labourers, masons etc. When they are not present, their female relatives, mother or wife, stand in for them. They have all at one point or the other been fined and arrested in the infrequent police raids. One of them said that they do not sell kassippu out of choice, but rather because they have to survive. He claimed that they only earn around Rs. 150/= per day and the rest goes to the businessman.

There is no observable ritual or ceremony in the consumption of kasippu, at least not in these sites. Men come there, not uncommonly alone, request a drink, pay the money and gulp from the glass sometimes while standing. Males can be observed moving to and from these places especially in the evenings. A few of them can be seen and heard singing the tunes of popular songs. When they get home, loud arguments, quarrels, wails, screams and shouts are heard from the houses. The noise of beatings and the smashing of pots and pans are not far behind. No youth and no female were detected as having consumed alcohol.

In the estate community, the resthouse in the middle of the village is the most important place for the sale of alcohol. The main customers are the estate workers. There is a notice here which specifies the times in which the resthouse can serve alcohol, but this is broken with impunity. Alcohol is sold in small glasses - not the "special" alcohol glasses, but the glasses which are used in the small eateries in Sri Lanka to sell tea - for amounts starting from Rs 20.

As far as the field assistant could observe, there are no rituals in the way these people consume the alcohol at this location. They come in hurriedly, either alone or in small groups, order while standing, pay the money and then gulp the drink down, while standing, with grimaces on their faces. They then quickly make their exit. It is more similar to the drinking of medicinal substance rather than a substance supposedly giving pleasure.

Kasippu sold within the village seems to be made in the surrounding villages or in the jungles. Alcohol consumption and its consequences seem to run from generation to generation. An example is Thiruchelvi, one of our informants. Her father died at the age of 40 due to drinking. Her mother has still not got his EPF money because they have not yet received his death certificate. She claims her husband also drinks toddy, kasippu and beer. Even though he barely works he joins with friends and drinks:

Sometimes I give him money to drink because I don't want him to cause any trouble. Since I have chosen to live with him, I have to bear up whatever is dished out. Drinking in the bar is ok, but sometimes he brings kasippu home and drinks it. I hate that, but what to do? I am unable to do anything about it.

Another of our informants is Punchi Mahaththaya. He smelled of alcohol while he was being interviewed in the daytime, but claimed to drink only twice or thrice a week. Normally he spends all his earning on drinking. It seems that he feels ashamed about his drinking habits. The excuse that he gives is that some months ago, his wife's jewellery was stolen, and after that he started to drink heavily. It was too much for him to handle emotionally. It seems that he does not worry about the feelings of his wife, who will return from abroad to find that her jewellery has disappeared, and the money she has sent home has been spent on alcohol.

Punchi Mahaththaya also drinks on credit. The bar owner knows that his wife is abroad and the money can be claimed. According to him when Punchi comes after work and sees some of his friends drinking, he automatically joins them, otherwise they might misunderstand. He claims that the bar is the cause of many social problems including his own:

If there was no bar here, certainly I would not drink. I can forget drinking and the people will also have less trouble. For example if I come back having earned 100 rupees, then on the way I see our boys drinking some beer there. Then I think why don't I also drink some beer. If I go for 30 days it will be 30 bottles of beer.

Not all women were reluctant to speak of the alcohol habits of their husbands. One of them said:

During the daytime he is like a cat and very quiet. But after 6 he drinks and comes home and starts shouting. I have even told him to stop at least for the children's sake because they might get spoilt, but he does not listen. Even though he makes money, most of the time he does not give me anything, and I have to forcibly take it from him. He seems to want to spend all the money on drinks.

It might be an indicator of the norms surrounding alcohol consumption that her husband was present during the interview, but he did not try to dispute these allegations. Instead he was very quiet.

In three villages the field assistant was unable to speak with a kasippu seller. The key informants were reluctant to introduce him to them. But in the fishing village the situation was different. It was easy to get in contact with people who sold kasippu. Furthermore, out of the ten informants three females did not drink alcohol. Out of the three women one sold kasippu and vegetables. The field assistant found that she talked as freely about her vegetable sales as about her kasippu sales, although she did try to give excuses for her kasippu business. This lady described her business like this:

"When we tell them how much we need, they bring it. I don't sell in the house as men come. There is a special room covered with wooden planks for this. If I bring 50 bottles I can get a profit of about 700 rupees. But I don't get the money at once. Some drink on credit. I have to allow this. My husband earns by cutting fish. He does not give one cent to me. Some times the police come. Last week they came. I had to pay 5000 rupees as fine. I pawned my chain to get the money. After 9 pm I do not sell. My husband also drinks from me. The villagers are not against my selling kasippu. I have about 10 to 15 regular customers. The sales increase around lunchtime. I don't sell to people who cause trouble after drinking. I have warned everyone that they should drink and then leave and not cause any problems for me. We have to be firm. Women do not come and scold me. They know that I do not force people to drink, and the men come because they want to. People might talk behind my back. But I know what I'm doing and I don't take men into the house.

From Friday afternoon the fishermen stay on land. Their work starts again on Sunday afternoon. These two days are their holiday and it is common to use alcohol to enjoy their holiday. Some drink on the beach. Some go to restaurants. For them, drinking alcohol is a great thing and a topic to talk about.

For these villagers alcohol is very much an integral part of their lives. This has been reported earlier too (Leitan 1995:26). According to her research, it is an accepted norm in these communites that men are entitled to relaxation through consumption of liquor. For it is felt by men as well as by women, that after being confined to a boat at sea for maybe days, and considering the hardships they are called upon to endure, drinking is permissible. One of our informants, a woman who is a small scale fish seller, put it like this:

"A fisherman will always drink. According to the amount of work they do, they must drink. They do heavy work."

In the Tamil village in Vavuniya, with displaced persons and natives, females are mainly involved in selling kasippu while males are primarily concerned with brewing. Our field assistant observed five places where women were selling kasippu, which is known by the name of "Kfir" in this area. Kasippu is a good trade with daily sales of around 100 – 125 bottles, which reach up to 600 – 700 bottles on festive occasions such as Deepavali. The price of a bottle is 100 rupees (compared to 120 rupees in neighbouring villages). One of the shops near the school is also selling "sealed arrack" on the sly.

The only setting where we did not experience any signs of alcohol consumption, was among the displaced Muslim population in Puttalam. There are no legal or illegal points of alcohol sale within the area. The Sinhala community neighbouring the area has the only known illicit alcohol selling stall. The Muslim residents usually do not go to that area. There were no individuals to be seen exhibiting behaviour usually associated with alcohol such as shouting obscenities, walking in staggered fashion etc. No-one certainly consumes alcohol in public in the area though there are several individuals who are known to consume alcohol in their homes.

Alcohol consumption on special occasions

Most of the negative norms about drinking seem to be connected to those few who use kasippu as a part of their daily life. Drinking on special occasions, like a wedding, is much more accepted. In a village wedding alcohol and meat are the essential items. People expect liquor to be served at a wedding. Most of the expenses of a wedding are for alcohol (arrack and kasippu), cigarettes and meat. All this will cost around 20,000 to 25,000 rupees. One informant suggested that nearly 25,000 rupees is spent on alcohol.

Several informants said that if there is no liquor at a wedding, the participation will be poor, and that there are people who do not go to a wedding if alcohol is not to be served. If there is no liquor, the value of the present, which is normally money, will be reduced. We were also told that some men will bring alcohol from outside and drink. They spend the money brought to give as the gift to buy arrack. A bottle costs about 300 rupees:

If 200 are invited they bring about 50 bottles of arrack. It costs them around 14,000 rupees. At some weddings if the hosts think it would be difficult to control the drinking they would avoid serving it. If a wedding is arranged with great financial difficulty they would serve kasippu instead of arrack.

Some might even eat, drink and enjoy and finally give an empty envelope and disappear. We even heard about someone who put an old lottery ticket in the envelope and gave it in a wedding where no alcohol was served.

When the field assistant in the fishing village asked his informants about a wedding without alcohol, they gave a sarcastic laugh at him. For them it was just a fantasy and something they had never heard of. They wondered whether it was even possible.

"If there's no alcohol, they will naturally be blamed. People might cause trouble. Normally people go to a wedding to drink. So it will be a big problem."

In several villages, alcohol consumption is also an integrated part of funerals. If the funeral society provides Rs. 5,000/= in assistance, most of it is spent on providing alcohol and other facilities for the supposed mourners who enjoy themselves at night by playing cards and gambling.

In the Tamil village in Vavuniya, drinking is also an integrated part of all special occasions, to such extent that even non-drinkers are socially influenced into drinking. Legal alcohol is bought for almost all special occasions. Some people, especially new settlers, run into debt by buying alcohol for such occasions.

Another special occasion that seems to include heavy alcohol consumption, is the Sinhala and Tamil New Year. In the Mihintale village we were told that during the months of February and March money circulation in the village is good. Therefore they celebrate New Year grandly. Whatever they save is spent on it. A large amount of the savings is spent on alcohol. Some more is spent on gambling, which is done there only for the New Year. Alcohol seems to be an unquestionable part of the celebration.

Norms about drinking and alcohol use

Norms and attitudes reside in the way people behave, and they can be expressed in interviews and conversations. In this section we will first describe the reasons that alcohol consumers give for their drinking. Then we look at the behaviour of the drinkers, and finally we describe how they are looked upon by the fellow villagers.

4.9.1 Excuses of people drinking

In most of our social settings the drinkers offered reasons or 'excuses' for drinking. One exception was the fishing village, where drinking alcohol was so obvious and natural that no excuses were needed.

One very common comment was that people regarded alcohol as a kind of medicine. The school teacher in the village in Vavuniya commented that people drink kasippu for any difficulty or illness. They say that in case of a headache if one drinks some kasippu and sleeps, he will be OK. In other villages we were told that some drink as a habit, some to forget their worries and some because there is nothing else to do. Several informants mentioned that people drink to get rid of their body aches after the days work. Relief from mental problems, was commonly mentioned as an excuse.

Several of our informants among the tea estate workers, also said that they work hard and it is good to drink alcohol for the tiredness of the body. One case is Ponnuchami the Laundry man, who says he is addicted to toddy. He says that his work is really hard and he drinks about two bottles every day to suppress the body pain and to sleep well. According to him he took up this habit only after starting this job. He sometimes borrows from the resthouse owner, and spends on average about Rs.50 per day on drinks.

Other heavy drinkers in the estate community gave more specific excuses for their drinking: the first born son died, a robber took the wife's jewellery etc. We have also seen that drinkers blame their situation on the existence of the bar. None of these excuses are very convincing, but they are still important as they reveal the norm structure. When excuses are needed, at least to an interviewer from outside, it is an indicator that the norms are not totally permissive.

Spending money on alcohol, can also be regarded as one form of conspicuous consump-tion. This concerns alcohol consumption both on special occasions as well as in everyday life. Of course none of our informant explicitly expressed it in this way, but for example in the village in Mihintale the field assistant found that most of the youths find the occasional use of alcohol as a way of showing you are a hero. They have learnt this by seeing how the youths in the forces or in the police or in private firms behave. When these young men come home for a vacation, they get together with their friends and share a bottle or two near the dam 'bunds'. The villagers accept it and see it as a way of recreation. Even the youths who work as labourers or who do farming, spend money on alcohol and cigarettes, when they do get money.

In most of our social settings, alcohol use also serves as a way of showing masculinity and ability. *"Nobody recognizes me, I have no place in this society. If I smoke and drink, people will see me as a man"*, said one of our informants in Katharagama. We were told that some people who drink want to show that there is nobody better than them in the village:

"I can do this and that. Who's there to go against me, I'm not afraid of anybody" is what they say.

"Once drunk they try to show how powerful they are", said one informant. In other words, alcohol seems to be an excuse for expressing position and strength. If a villager talks against a man who has drunk and is shouting, *"Why should you care whether I drink or not, who are you to tell me, mind your own business"* are the remarks he would get according to our informants in Katharagama.

4.9.2 Drunken behaviour

In several of our villages it was clear that the kasippu drinkers were somewhat ashamed of their habit. When they met strangers on the roadside they often behaved in a guilty fashion with some of them covering their mouths in an effort to stem the odour. It was also observed that the villagers look at them in an unfriendly manner with dislike and usually do not converse with them. Especially females avoid interaction with them when they are drunk.

The fact that the kasippu-drinkers avoid being noticed by others, can be seen as an indicator that there are social norms condemning their drinking. We were told that people drink alcohol from the places that sell it. They go in quietly and come out trying not to be noticed by others. There are though some instances where people who are intoxicated on kasippu use the fact to make a noise.

We have earlier mentioned that intoxication is used as an excuse for distancing oneself from a powerless and suppressed situation. This is also confirmed by the behaviour of the drunkards. It is revealed that they sometimes pretend to be more drunk than they actually are, at least it seemed they controlled their drunken behaviour. We were told that some drunkards keep quiet while passing a sacred or important place but start shouting again once it is passed. They shout not because they are drunk but to show that they have drunk. Another informant told how the shouting drunkards shut up for just a couple of minutes when they pass a house owned by a village leader.

4.9.3 Norms surrounding alcohol consumption

In the fishing village the norms surrounding alcohol consumption seemed to be very permissive. When the field assistant questioned his informants 'Is it essential to drink alcohol when you are a boy?' they replied that *'When you are a fisherman you have to drink alcohol'*. In the fishing village people do not give information to the police about kasippu but they give information about other drugs being sold. According to the villagers this is also not so much to reduce drugs from the village but to go against a rival.

Among the tea estate workers there seemed to be norms expressing that consuming alcohol is part of the male role. One of our informants said that if his friends were drinking, he had to join them, or they would "misunderstand".

There is also a certain minority on the tea estate which does not consume alcohol. They argue that alcohol is the root cause of many evils that characterize life on the estate. However, the person who does not drink is affected by it because he has to serve alcohol during special occasions whether he likes it or not, because of tradition. They put up with it and prefer to leave things as they are, for what they say is the fear of unnecessary quarrels. One of our informants at the estate who never tasted alcohol himself, told us that when very close relatives come visiting, he entertains them with drinks.

Villagers have a habit of giving excuses for the things done and said after drinking alcohol, and this goes for most of our villages. There also seems to be a strong and clear acceptance regarding alcohol use. Behaviour that would never be accepted by a sober man, is ignored or laughed at if the person is drunk. Very often even the non-drinkers try to find an excuse for the ones who drink. There are many who do not drink or are against alcohol. The villagers respect them, but when compared to those who drink, they are less spoken about. This had led to the impression that drinking alcohol is a way of earning some credit ('marks') or status. Another informant said:

Drinking and shouting is his habit. So we should look at it in a very delicate way and forgive him.

In Katharagama there seemed to be different and rather contradictory norms about alcohol use in the villages we visited.

Many villagers say drunkards are seen as useless and foolish, both because their behaviour is foolish, and because it is a foolish way to spend their money. The image seems particularly strong regarding the few who drink kasippu more or less daily:

Twenty to twenty-five villagers get together at these places in the evenings to drink. When they are drunk they search for trouble. They bring up long lost misunderstandings and start fights. When they are drunk they cannot even recognize their parents. They think of themselves as thugs. The villagers regard them as fools and avoid interactions with them.

It also appears that the norms and the reactions operate mainly against the uncontrolled drinking and especially the annoying behaviour. It is not the alcohol use as such the villagers react against. At the same time some people seem to think that if you do not smoke a cigarette or drink alcohol you will not be respected by their society:

If you don't smoke or if you don't drink and if you don't enjoy life the society will think you are useless. Therefore I must behave like them.

Similar norms were revealed by the fact that people were reluctant to react against the illicit alcohol outlets. When asked whether they tried to do anything regarding this, one informant replied:

No need. Why do we want unnecessary problems? Let's assume that we start a campaign to collect signatures to remove the bar. They will put the signature here and go and tell the bar owner what is happening. This will lead to unnecessary problems. It is better if the government or someone like that does it. As for the resthouse, there is not much of a problem. There is an order that says that they can sell only after 2 pm[11].

The permissive norms about alcohol use, can also be seen in the fact that alcohol is used as a lubricant to get things done. Particularly among the workers at the tea estate, we heard several stories about this. If there is a funeral, alcohol has to be given to the grave-diggers. It has also been used as a kind of bribe. Our key informant told this story:

If we give the kangani some alcohol, then he will write our name as having worked in the estate. If one gives the field officer a quarter to half a bottle, then when he records the tea leaves he will increase it by 5 or 10 kg. Mostly in this country everything happens with alcohol.

Alcohol is also used as an incentive by the political parties during the election times.

During election times they take people to tie up flags and banners and to put up posters. Mostly people go for alcohol and food only. I have also gone like that. I have taken people as well. If they are given alcohol then the people are very happy. Before drinking they will be alright. After they drink they will tear the posters of others and problem will arise.

To sum up, it seems that the norms about alcohol consumption are rather permissive in most of our villages. The drunkards are tolerated, and so are the kasippu sellers. If the drunkards drink and shout, the villagers generally stay quiet. And the people who sell kasippu are not openly condemned. One informant told us:

What they are doing is wrong, but even though the majority of society are badly affected by this, he tries to look after his family from it. So we must look at the issue sympathetically.

Economic consequences of alcohol use

As documented in the chapter based on quantitative data, some men spend all their earnings, and occasionally even more, on alcohol. Also in our village studies we heard stories about how very little money was left for the wife and children of daily drinkers.

In the village in Mihintale our field assistant noticed that when he asked 'whether you are drinking alcohol', all of a sudden there was a change in their behaviour and a smile came to their face. The use of alcohol and the positive attitudes towards it have caused most of the money of the village to be spent on it. This is a major reason for the poverty of the village, the field assistant concluded. To some extent this seems to be a consequence of modernization and of the increase in the number of youths leaving the village and clustering in the towns. This has led to an increase also in the number of villagers who think highly of the use of beer and arrack and of smoking cigarettes. There is an increase in the number of occasions when alcohol is used as a way of saying thank you and as a way of showing happiness.

In the Tamil village in Vavuniya, with displaced persons and natives, the consequences of alcohol use can be seen on the economy of the villagers, and on the life conditions of children and women. In other social settings we have seen that family fathers and providers spend on alcohol a large part of their small earnings. In this village the dry rations from the government is an important part of survival for many families. When our field assistant observed the handing out of the rations, he saw that in a short period of around an hour at least five individuals who collected the 'dry ration' sold their goods at low prices to the grocery shop owners. When queried as to what they will do with the money, bystanders replied,

"Wait a little, will you! You will see those people coming back after consuming kasippu".

The impression of our field assistant in Vavuniya was that most of the money earned or saved is spent on alcohol. The reason for this is the various habits and the various norms created for the benefit of the drinkers. Even though people think that alcohol drinking is a popular and great thing they show some dislike of the people who sell it. They think that the seller or producer is doing wrong. Some of the villagers wish that kasippu was no more in the village but at the same time they are proud to say that it is from their village that alcohol is sent to the nearby villages. Even if they are opposed to the kasippu sale, they are happy that they have the leading position compared to the other villages, and they were rather proud in saying that everybody, even those from other villages, knew "their" kasippu-selling woman.

In the village in Katharagama, as in several other places, we were also told that some go straight after work to drink kasippu. They spend all of the day's earning on kasippu and go home 'when the pocket is empty'. Thus the economic consequences of alcohol use are intolerably heavy for the minority that drinks kasippu every day.

The amount of money spent on alcohol in weddings and other occasions, also effects poverty and development. As we have already mentioned, most of the villagers borrow money for weddings planning to pay back with the money they receive as gifts, but the amount collected is often not enough. Sometimes the lender takes over land owned by the debtor.

So even people who are not so well off financially, take loans and have a grand wedding. To get the goodwill of the villagers they serve at least kasippu. Some serve legal alcohol. If they are financially well off, they bring a large number of bottles. We were told that there are some, even if they do not have money, who want to show that they are rich. They are mainly uneducated people, we were told. They have their weddings grandly and make it a point to serve much alcohol at it.

Production and sale of illicit alcohol is a source of income for some villagers. We were told that as the people have no other way of earning a living they get involved in this sort of business: *"We need to survive. We can't rob so we sell kasippu and live"*. Even if it is the women of the village that are the main victims of the men's drinking, women are also involved in the kasippu business. At least in some of the outlets, it was the woman of the house who sold kasippu.

Social consequences of alcohol use

From other parts of the world we know that many accidents such as drowning result from alcohol use. This is also the case in the village of Awissawella. In the valley that borders the village runs a moderate sized waterway. At one point it deepens to a large pool

Thepool recently claimed another victim. Despite its deadliness it continues to remain a favourite location for people to travel from far, take alcohol and swim.

known as "Leel wala". This spot has claimed the lives of at least seven people in the recent past as stated by the locals. In the month of August alone three youths died at the same spot. During the time that the field assistant was staying in the village this pool claimed another victim, a 21 year old male. Despite its obvious deadliness it continues to remain a favourite location for travellers from far to come and consume alcohol and bathe. All those who drowned at this spot, in the opinion of the villagers, were those who had consumed large amounts of alcohol. They further claimed that the reason why they could not come ashore was because they were "drunk". Of course despite this the large majority of people who come there do consume alcohol and return home unharmed!

We have already shown how alcohol use has economic consequences, and how it complicates the already very difficult situation of women. Unpleasant behaviour in public places was a repeated theme in several interviews in most social settings:

Women cannot go out alone here at night. After drinking, the villagers create trouble and mischief. They will pick fights with those who walk on the roads and assault them.

Fathers' drunkenness also has consequences for the school attendance of the children. The principal and the teachers at the village school in Vavuniya referred to children who did not go to school because the parents were fighting due to alcohol use. Children said that due to the fighting there was no cooking, so they could not come to school. Other children had told people that their drunken father had assaulted and chased their mother. *"We were scared, so we couldn't sleep"*, the children had said.

One consequence of alcohol consumption in the wet zone use was that young females were excluded from funerals. Males stay awake at the funeral through the night, and heavy alcohol consumption is often an accompaniment. Many outsiders are said to come to the village during funerals, and frequently fights take place during these events, after consuming alcohol.

In the fishing village that we mentioned earlier that alcohol drinking was regarded a normal issue and not something to be ashamed of. But even there we met a few who think this is a problem for society. Most people regard alcohol as something which leads to fights, conflicts, and hostility among villagers. Smoking cannabis is believed to cause calmness, quietness, and understanding. The field assistant thought that this village has more fights and conflicts due to alcohol compared to other rural villages.

The fact that the heavy drinkers represent a nuisance both to their families and to the village, is described in several settings and in various ways:

It is not difficult to walk on the streets alone, but after 8 at night it is not safe as there are drunkards on the roads.

There are families who have been mentally suppressed due to the drunkenness of the husband. Some wives tolerate it while others cannot and they have divorced. There are a lot of family conflicts due to this. There have also been several murders due to the drunkenness.

Murder is of course the most extreme form of violence. But even in cases that are less dramatic, those who drink are generally seen as a nuisance to their homes. Again and again we were told that there is no harmony among the members of the families with men who drink. Their drinking is a problem both to the wife and the children.

According to our informants, husbands with their wives abroad are particularly vulnerable to problematic alcohol use. This is generally attributed to the fact that they receive money from the Middle East, and that they are no longer subject to the social control that the wife represents.

Domestic violence

A frequent accompaniment of alcohol consumption that we have mentioned already, and that we heard of in all our villages other than the Muslim settlement in Puttalam, is violence against women and children. Gender based violence should of course not be regarded as only a result of drinking, but also as a problem in itself.

4.12.1 A case story from Vavuniya

The most dramatic evidence of such violence in our data is from the village in Vavuniya. One particular incident happened while our field assistant was visiting the village. Nallamma was 28 years old and the mother of five children. One night as her husband came home drunk and attacked his wife severely in front of the children. When one of the children attempted to shout, this child was banged against the wall. When the other children looked scared, he had told all the children to stand against the wall, then put his hands around Nallamma's neck and tried to strangle her. She fainted and the husband assumed she was dead. He then took the body and threw it into jungle behind the house. After that he left and the children started shouting. People came running and found out that Nallamma was still alive and took her to the hospital.

Our field assistant was rather surprised that no one, neither the neighbours nor Nallamma herself, complained to the police. The field assistant heard that she made others promise that they would not report this to the police. The reason she gave was that she was worried about what would happen to the children if something happened to her and her husband too was sent to jail. At the end of his stay the field assistant heard it said that Nallamma had died in hospital.

4.12.2 High prevalence of domestic violence

This could be seen as a rare and special incident if it was not for the fact that similar, although less dramatic stories were recounted by all our field assistants. The prevalence of domestic violence is clearly very high. This is also documented in other studies. According to International Planned Parenthood Foundation, violence against women is increasing in Sri Lanka[12]. As the number of battered women has become increasingly high, a project was set up called 'Media Watch'. From January to June 1998 'Media Watch' carried out a survey based on monitoring newspapers and analysing the number of cases related on violence perpetrated by a family member or within the home and then comparing these numbers with general violence cases not based on domestic matters. The purpose of this exercise was to monitor the number of Sri Lankan women subjected to domestic violence. Of course such a study only reveals what is called the tip of the iceberg, but during these five months the newspapers reported 52 cases where a woman was murdered by a domestic perpetrator, and 44 cases of domestic assault.

According to a WHO report, among women aged 15-44 years gender based violence accounts for more death and disability than, cancer, malaria, traffic injuries or war put together. Evidence from Sri Lanka showed that 60 % of 200 women interviewed said they were beaten by their partners, 51 of the women said their partner used a weapon during the physical assault (Sonali 1990). In a report published by WHO, no other county showed a higher percentage of beaten wives.

But since mild forms of wife-beating appear commonplace, there is reason to believe that there is much underreporting, that the number may even be higher than 60%. In a study from south India, an anthropologist encountered several cases of domestic violence during her stay in the villages (Rao 1997). Many men and women admitted to it in informal conversations, often claiming that it was justified if the wife did not "behave". However, in the context of the survey interview, only 22% of the women admitted to having been physically assaulted by their husbands. In that study it was evident that only the women for whom beating was a serious and chronic problem admitted it. Thus, while wife-beating is an everyday affair for many women, they do not consider it a "problem" worthy of being characterized as assault unless it is severe.

4.12.3 Violence and masculinity

Violence against women was found in almost all the social settings from which we gathered data in our study. For instance in the fishing village, our field assistant reported that women seemed to have the opportunity to think and live independently. Even if her husband does not earn anything, the wife is capable of finding money somehow. But this is sometimes a problem for the men. They try to suppress women and because of this there are numerous family conflicts. There also seemed to be a widespread acceptance of domestic violence. Together with talk about sex, this is a hot topic in the alcohol drinking settings of the village, and the men even boasted about hitting women. As we noticed in Colombo this seemed to be a way of expressing masculine norms and identity.

As mentioned earlier, in the fishing village people live very close together. The houses are small, usually with only one room. The effect of what we could call the porosity of a life in poverty is clearly visible. The field assistant noted that small children are exposed frequently to an environment where parents both fight and have sex.

That this is problem not only for the women, but also for the children, was evident from our data from the village in Awissawella. There a mother was standing on the roadside with her two school-going children after having been chased out by her husband who had consumed alcohol. She complained that he had burnt all the school equipment of the children.

In Awissawella it seemed that most men, having consumed alcohol before reaching home, initiate disputes with their family members. This usually involves physical altercations with their wives and on some occasions their parents (there was one instance of a father and son assaulting each other after consuming alcohol). We also found that the attitudes surrounding men's alcohol use are connected to norms about masculinity and femininity. The school teacher of this village told us:

"Most of the women in the village do everything for their men. If they don't do so, the men will hit them. Even if they hit and wound them, still they do all the work. They do not oppose them".

4.12.4 Norms about non interference

There are also strong norms about non interference in domestic violence. *'This is their issue and problem'*, one informant said. The field assistant noted that from several houses the loud noises of quarrels, disputes, crying and wailing emanate after nightfall. No outsiders attempt to interfere. As one informant put it the cause for most of the night fights are due to either the dinner being not ready when the husband returns or a delay in preparing hot water for a wash.

Similar norms and attitudes were found among the estate workers. In our data from the estate community, we have the story of Ramiah. He was said to be in his late thirties but appeared much older. Having been pointed out by the key informant as a heavy consumer of alcohol, the field assistant scheduled an interview with him. The interview never took place, because Ramiah passed away suddenly on the night before the appointment. He had come home drunk as usual but had suddenly collapsed. The family and others being used to his actions had shrugged it off as due to the effects of alcohol. Later realizing he was in real difficulty, they took him to the Estate Medical Officer who ordered that he be immediately taken to the hospital. However he was dead on admission.

A few days after her husband's funeral the field assistant had a chance to speak to the widow. She said her husband was a nice man and a hard working guy. She had married him when she was just 17 and without her parents' knowledge. She excused her late husband saying that their first born was a son and he had died. Ramiah had started drinking partly due to this and partly due to his friends. He was a character who liked to impress people. Everybody who spoke about him said that he was a nice man despite his drinking. He would help anyone in need said the widow, but she also mentioned the fighting and violence:

My husband used to fight with me and assault me after drinking. He listened to something somebody said and hit me on the head. I once had a "split" head. I had to have seven stitches. I went to the police and they made peace between us and sent me back. I have two children. What to do? Where to go? I thought about that and just lived like that. I couldn't go back to my parents. I married him according to my wish.

According to his wife even though he spent most of his money drinking they had never starved. He somehow went to work and brought stuff, but never money because of his drinking. He never gave money to his wife and she always had to take it from his pocket. He used to beat up his wife quite often and even his kids. His daughter is prone to fits, and his wife claimed she has constant chest pain because of his beatings. He had even broken her head with the coconut scrapper once and the case had been reported to the police[13]. His relations had forsaken him because he was a drunkard. 'Even though this man was a good person, he turned into a monster after drinking'. The field assistant found it amazing to hear such a person still being called a good person. But the family and community had decided that all he did was beyond him and was due purely to the alcohol. Ramiah was considered to be the victim rather than the abuser.

But Ramiah was not the only man beating his wife in this community. Another informant was Ponnuchami the Laundry man, who says he is an addict to toddy. He says that his work is really hard and he drinks about two bottles every day to suppress the body pain and to sleep well. Ponnuchami's story is also illustrative of the norms regarding domestic violence[14], and what some estate workers feel regarding beating their wives when they confront the men about the way money is spent. Ponnuchami's wife often confronts him often about his drinking. He did not seem ashamed when he reported that he had beaten her several times. Proudly he claimed that he did not like people telling him what to do. He says people at the village say that Ponnuchami is a nice guy only his family is spoilt. He appears not to care about the fact that he beats his wife and says that he can do whatever he wants with his life. According to him it was his wife that was to blame when she was beaten.

There is also a certain minority among the estate workers who do not consume alcohol. They argue that alcohol is a root cause of many evils that characterize life in the estate. But even the person who does not drink avoids interfering with the drunken behaviour and the domestic violence in his neighbourhood. One such person told us:

There are people who drink, beat their wives and shout. But we do not interfere in their issues because we will never be able to live in peace after that. A war will break out if we say something against it. So we have to tolerate it, but it is so bad that we can't sleep in the nights sometimes.

Similar views were expressed by other informants:

Some people shout a lot after drinking. If we ask why they are shouting, there will be a big problem. Therefore we think, let him shout and we close our doors and wait. Sometimes we can't sleep at night. They assault their wife and children. Nobody goes and asks what is your problem. If we tell them that we have to sleep at night, they reply that we put the TV and radio through the night, and doesn't that too make noise.

What we see here are strong norms of non-interference in other people's lives, their drinking, and their behaviour inside and outside their homes. Violence is common, and it is accepted. Physical and psychological abuse, which if it occurred in a public place would be condemned, is tolerated by society merely because it takes place within a family or domestic setting. The existence of a family or domestic relationship has given perpetrators the 'right' to abuse others, whether it be a spouse, a partner, elderly relative or child. This is almost a social right. And alcohol allows the violent expression of this right with little personal misgivings or guilt.

4.12.5 Alcohol and violence

In our own study, as in several others, women see the connection between men's drinking and their violence very clearly. Also in the Indian study mentioned earlier, most women who were beaten complained that the problem was exacerbated by the drunken fits of their husbands. Sometimes drunkenness acted as a catalyst, in the sense that arguments that would otherwise have passed uneventfully would turn violent if the husband was drunk. Drunken husbands would also assault their wives without any provocation. One middle-aged woman quoted in this study compared having an alcoholic husband to "being in jail", where "you cannot do anything freely because anything you do may provoke your husband into beating you".

Another study from South India is examining the prevalence of domestic violence in a fishing community in Kerala, a community that seems to have much in common with our own fishing village in Gampaha (cf. Busby 1999). Violence there seems inevitable and men are not usually seen as to blame. In that study too, the role of alcohol is evident. The author of that study, an anthropologist, is critical of the local understanding – which has led to a focus on alcohol as the root of the problem, with men still perceived to be personally not at fault.

In that study, like in our own, when the women described their husbands' violence, there was a sense in which the violence seemed almost detached from his person. It was seen as a force of nature, something about which you could do nothing. And in the community, the blame for a man's violent behaviour towards his wife went very frequently not to him at all but to her. This study also confirms the finding in our own study, that people usually don't interfere with marital quarrels. Even female neighbours would stand against the beaten woman, and say, 'well she must have deserved it, she had a bad tongue' and so on. In our own study we found people saying about a woman who was beaten almost to death by her husband, that she had been spoilt in her childhood.

Alcohol and Poverty

Notes

1. We were told that bout 30% had received Swarnabhumi Deeds by President Premadhasa.

2. This is confirmed by a study of two fishing villages in the Negombo area (Leitan 1995:32-34). In her study Tressie Leitan found a marked lack of interest in education, which seemed to contrast strangely with the situation in the urban sector as well as in the rural agricultural sector. She found around half of the villagers had studied up to grade 5, and 8% had no schooling at all

3. According to a study done by FAO, 25% of all women in Negombo, Chilaw and Kalpitya on the West coast are estimated to be engaged in fishing-related activities. Source: http://www.fao.org/sd/WPdirect/WPre0112.htm

4. Cf. Leitan (1995:27) who found a pattern of spending and a lack of interest in saving that could be attributed to observable attitudes in the fishing villages. She describes a tendency to spend the day's earnings, for after all, there is so much fish in the sea which could be caught tomorrow. According to her, this attitude could also be tied up with the Christian belief in God's providence and faith in what tomorrow can bring.

5. According to an article in the Indian magazine Frontline, the literacy rate in the estate sector in Sri Lanka is only 76.9 percent. The article describes how previous generations of estate workers grew up illiterate, as education was systematically denied them. Some estates had schools, but only up to the primary level. It was only from 1977 that high schools were introduced in the estates. Today these schools are seen as departure lounges to the world outside. Source: Subramania, N. (2001).

6. A Dutch study of the situation on the tea estates, shows that women from 16 years do the hard physical labour of plucking tea from 8 a.m. until 5 p.m. daily and are responsible, before and after work, for all domestic tasks. Men working on the estate do not pluck tea (considered women's work), but instead prepare the land, apply fertilizer, spray pesticides, prune, work in the factory, act as drivers, or are field supervisors of groups of pluckers. Most of this work is done in the morning and after lunch men are free. Men never help with domestic chores although women and girls, already burdened with a heavy work load, spend 4-6 hours per day fetching water. Men earn the same amount for half a day's work as women earn for tea plucking. Source:Van der Laan, Anita (1998).Other studies have found that that when men collect the family's estate income and find it getting larger, they feel less need to work and so they labour less on the estate. But women, on the other hand, continue to be engaged in plantations. Source: http://www.fao.org/sd/WPdirect/WPre0112.htm

7. Employer Provident Fund is based on compulsory contributions from the employers. When the employer retires, the whole sum is paid out at once in one sum.

8. Subramanian (op.cit.) describes how it earlier was unthinkable for a young boy, or especially a young woman, to venture outside the tea estate on which they were born, to make a living. Today, teenage girls commute considerable distances to garment factories, to exchange the drudgery of plucking two leaves and a bud from the tea bushes for the monotony of sewing buttons on to shirts.

9. The village is also described in a study done by D. Abeysekera of IDPs in Sri Lanka (Abeysekera 2002:27). There it is categorized as a temporary relocated village. According to Abeysekera there are 186 temporary relocated families living in the village together with about 100 families who are the native residents as well as another 100 internally displaced families who are living with friends or relatives. Most of the relocated families are from the very next villages only a few kilometres away.

10. This impression is confirmed by the findings of Tressie Leitan (Leitan 1995:24-25). She found that much was spent on expensive clothes, for children as well as for adults. Her interviewers came across a family which had just spent Rs. 2000/- for a dress for a six year old child. Another major item of expenditure described in her study of two fishing villages, was tobacco and alcohol for the men. Around half of the men spent more that Rs. 1000/- for these items.

11. According to the field assistant this rule imposed by the estate management is disregarded.

12. Source: http://www.ippf.org/resource/gbv/ma98/2.htm#2_6

13. Sri Lanka currently has no single law on domestic violence. A victim of domestic abuse would need to make use of the criminal law or make a creative use of the fundamental rights provisions to seek relief. So far the fundamental rights provisions have not been used to deal with domestic violence. Source: http://www.lawandsocietytrust.org/LSTReview.asp?VolNo=17&List=True

14. The term 'domestic violence' has been heavily critizised, because it tends to neutralize and hide both who is assaulting whom, and the harsh impact of this form of abuse. Other terms used in international literature, are 'violence against women' and 'gender-based violence'.

Conclusions

Alcohol

5.1.1 The role of alcohol

One question addressed in this study was the role of alcohol in different social settings in Sri Lanka. The second was the extent to which alcohol creates, perpetuates or worsens poverty or hinders development.

As regards the first question, our study showed that alcohol plays a large and important role in all the social settings we looked at other than in the Muslim community in Puttalam. Alcohol, and the consequences of alcohol use, influence greatly the everyday life of poor people. Not only are the lives severely affected of those who drink, but, perhaps even more, the lives of others such as their wives and children. Even the households where no one touches alcohol are heavily influenced by the alcohol drinking. We saw also that people are allowed to behave in obnoxious ways after using alcohol. Behaviour that would not at all have been accepted of a sober man is met with forgiveness and a smile if the man is drunk.

If the norms about alcohol in everyday life are permissive, the norms about alcohol on special occasions are prescriptive. We have heard numerous stories about how a wedding without alcohol is unthinkable, and about the severe sanctions against people who dare to go against the norms and, for instance, try to arrange a wedding without alcohol.

To return to a concept introduced in chapter 1, we too found that the meanings that people ascribe to alcohol can be linked to status along both horizontal and vertical dimensions. It serves to integrate as well as to separate people. Along the horizontal dimension, we did see that drinking can be an expression of group membership, as when the tea estate worker felt that he could not pass the bar where his friends were drinking without joining them. Just passing them would mean excluding himself from a group to which he wanted to belong. And we saw how the young men coming from remote villages to the boarding houses in Colombo, pay a high price for the membership in the male drinking groups. The decision to drink, of how much to drink, and of which beverage, and the choice of whom to drink with, all become means for claiming and living out an identity (cf. Room 2002:36).

Along the vertical dimension, we saw how disobedience and resistance may be communicated through drinking. In Katharagama we were told that some people who drink want to show that there is nobody better than them in the village, as if they directly or indirectly are expressing: *"I can do this and that, who's there to stop me. I'm not afraid of anybody"*[1]. They are setting themselves apart through their drinking.

The vertical dimension is also visible when people place themselves in a situation of lifelong debt, because they choose to celebrate a wedding or another special occasion with such large amounts of alcohol. It seems that celebrations like that include an element of distancing oneself from the poverty of everyday life. The show off element is important both to the family, who have to live with the debt afterwards, and to the rest of the village.

We have described drinking patterns, drinking situations and the consequences of alcohol use. There are however, four aspect of alcohol consumption that we should highlight particularly. That is the money spent on alcohol, the role of alcohol in making the socially unacceptable acceptable, the subjective effect of alcohol, and 'fun' and illicit alcohol.

5.1.2 Money spent on alcohol

Most people do recognize that calculating the rupee cost of reported alcohol consumption is too narrow a measure of the burden of alcohol. It is recognized to be too narrow even as a measure of the economic impact of alcohol. But how much money people actually spend on alcohol, especially in relation to their incomes, is still worth calculating.

In many studies and censuses the money spent on alcohol and various other things that people buy are surveyed and calculated. There are several studies in Sri Lanka too assessing the 'economic impact' of alcohol, which refer to the proportion of people's income that is spent on alcohol (ADIC- FORUT 1998).[2] Such studies report the expenditure on alcohol in the past week or on a typical day and so on.

Our study suggests that the calculation of expenditure on alcohol is heavily underestimated, and this due to factors beyond the deliberate and unwitting 'underestimation' of costs in self reports.

In discussions with all of the groups sampled we found a highly significant 'subsidizing' of the costs of alcohol by those who drank little or no alcohol. People who don't themselves consume alcohol contribute significantly to the costs of alcohol purchases for special events. Payments for others' alcohol use are not usually included when expenditures on alcohol are calculated or studied. The cost of alcohol for which others pay does not get accounted for by the consumer either. So a large amount of alcohol expenditure is not recognized when studies of alcohol related expenses are studied. This is because the users too don't count the expenses of others who subsidize their alcohol purchases while the people who pay for others' alcohol don't count that money either.

Much of this 'uncounted' expense is for alcohol purchased for special occasions. For some, these special occasions arise rather frequently. Many of the young people in the boardings and the three-wheeler stands reported such events at least once a week. Community residents too described the same phenomenon. We also saw how money was taken away from non-users in a rather forcible way too, possibly even as a way of keeping them economically equal.

Another expenditure that is not counted, is money that is not considered part of 'regular' income. Most illegal income is readily spent on alcohol (or other drugs) because the money is not 'real'. Sudden windfalls too go this way. Gifts and other extra income that people get often gets channelled solely for alcohol purchases and other accompaniments.

Even non-celebratory or non-event based alcohol use (namely regular or day-to-day use) is subsidized in many ways. Irregular income, such as through lotteries, bribes, fraud and cheating, gets into the alcohol pool. Different individuals in a drinking group contribute in this way on different days. 'Loans' taken and not repaid, forcible donations gathered from various sources and collections for alleged good deeds are channels through which regular drinking too gets subsidized by people who are not in the drinking group. A large contributor to the regular alcohol purchases of heavy daily drinkers are their wives who contribute part of their earnings for the man's alcohol, so as to keep the peace within the home.

Perhaps much the larger 'unaccounted' (or, more strictly, 'uncounted') expense of this kind is for alcohol served at weddings and 'big girl' parties. This, in relation to people's income, is huge money. Because this is a 'once-off' cost, the amounts involved are never added to the alcohol expenses calculation, but a family may spend the rest of their lifetime paying off debts, or forever paying interest, incurred for wedding expenses. A sizeable part of these expenses is for alcohol.

Our impression is that this contribution from 'invisible' sources that never get accounted for is substantial. It may even amount to more than half of all expenditures on alcohol. This quantum is not captured in any econometric analysis of the expenditures on alcohol. Neither those who subsidize the alcohol purchase nor those who consume the free alcohol recognize this money as an expenditure on alcohol. There is accompanying expense on tobacco, other substances and accompaniments that go with alcohol consumption which do not get tallied as an alcohol cost but is nonetheless an alcohol-related cost.

Conclusion: Research on alcohol expenditures have to take note of this huge cost that informants never report - because they themselves do not notice it.

5.1.3 The role of alcohol in making the socially unacceptable acceptable

A repeated finding from all our social settings was that of people talking openly and light-heartedly, in the drinking setting, of behaviours that would be considered vicious or nasty in other settings. This is different from the usual permission to have 'time-out' or 'freedom from usual norms' during alcohol consumption. What happens here is that people can talk openly while 'drunk' about flouting norms of decency during times that they were *not* 'drunk'. The 'permission' to break usual rules is extended, retrospectively, to things that were done in the non-intoxicated state. This extension is achieved by using the 'freedom from usual norms' attitude in the alcohol setting to boastingly reveal norm breaking conducted in the non-intoxicated state.

It is permissible to talk, while intoxicated, about behaviour that would be frowned upon elsewhere. By openly proclaiming, say, grabbing a chain from a frail old lady, the perpetrator is able somehow to make it okay. Because it is now out in the open, safely during the 'disinhibited' drinking session, it gets cleansed. The mechanism is often to make a joke or humorous statement about the event. In laughing about it the group affirms that the act was not really so bad.

Many informants report that the open expression, in drinking situations, of what is normally considered unacceptable or vicious, changes the norms of their group as a whole. The open airing (even amounting to boasts) of behaviours that were considered bad or low, somehow makes them less bad or embarrassing. What was previously considered nasty is now 'cleansed' through this process, so the 'lowered' standards of the alcohol drinking session 'spill-over' to affect the standards of society as a whole. 'We can break the rules because they are a joke anyway, as we learnt at the drinking session yesterday'.

We discussed how it is possible, through the continued operation of this dynamic, to make what was the previously unaccepted now gradually accepted and later even admired. It is also possible to see how the process can apply to increasingly unacceptable levels of behaviour. Such a process can hypothetically lead, given sufficient time, to a state where there may be nothing left that is considered unacceptable.

Conclusion: This finding is relevant to 'development' that goes beyond just the economic. A society that allows its rules to be broken in the alcohol setting risks losing those rules altogether.

5.1.4 The subjective effect of alcohol

The way people evaluated the subjective experience of alcohol was strikingly different in different settings. It appears that social influences have a strong bearing on the subjective effect produced by alcohol and on how it is rated.

A significant difference was found, for example, between the younger alcohol users of the two overcrowded urban communities. In one, alcohol use is rated universally by young persons to be highly enjoyable. In the second, few younger users were convinced that the effect of alcohol is indeed an enjoyable experience.

An apparent paradox was why, or how, a large majority of occasional users in this setting, who said that they did not like the effect of alcohol, still continued to drink. They all said that they drank to conform, but it wasn't clear how nearly all could claim to be drinking to conform, and not for enjoyment of the alcohol use *per se*.

If nearly all find alcohol use not a really enjoyable experience and nearly all were drinking to conform, what was the force that made alcohol use the 'conformist' behaviour? Certainly not the enjoyment if their self reported subjective experience is to be believed. The persons questioned said that it was the done or expected thing. The implication is that the feeling that one should take alcohol in fun situations came from the wider environment – not necessarily from the members of the alcohol-using group.

Conclusion: It will be useful to study the proportion of people in different drinking occasions who say that they enjoy the effect of alcohol. What the attributes are of those who enjoy the experience and those who do not are worth studying too. The practical implications for work on preventing alcohol-related harm are major.

5.1.5 'Fun' and illicit alcohol

Drinking occasions are often meant for fun and enjoyment, but we hardly found any reports of 'fun' with illicit alcohol use. Why illicit alcohol users are not afforded the privilege of making the drinking a merry occasion is unclear. In the urban and rural settings described, in our report and in the 'Thotalanga' community of Sri Lanka (described in 'Illicit Alcohol' - Abeysinghe 2002) all seem not to allow 'fun' with illicit alcohol. People come, buy their kasippu and quickly drink it or simply carry it away. The study from Thotalanga reported that the illicit brew contained the same chemical or molecule – ethyl alcohol.

The easiest possible explanation is that the illegality of the brew does not permit people to openly sit around consuming it, so there is no possibility of building up rituals around the consumption. Nor is there much symbolic 'status' value built up around kasippu. It is cheap and the poorest folk drink it.

When consumers display signs of intoxication, they are permitted the liberty of suspending their 'inhibitions'. Some kasippu users therefore do shout abuse at others as they walk back home intoxicated, but no real 'fun' is linked to kasippu use. Perhaps illicit alcohol has still not penetrated the social barrier enough to become an accepted or normal ritual.

Conclusion: There is a stark difference between the effects of consuming ethyl alcohol in different packaging – kasippu versus legal arrack or beer. The example here should be helpful in explaining the social modulation of alcohol effects. The part that chemistry plays in determining the subjective effect of alcohol and alcohol-related behaviour may be smaller than we assume.

Poverty

5.2.1 Dimensions of poverty

Through the descriptions of our social settings, we have shown that poverty is a complex phenomenon. As we argued in our introductory chapter, poverty is not just one thing, and it is not just a question of income. A more comprehensive approach should not only cover economical and material poverty, but also several kinds of social poverty. If we look to analyze poverty based on participatory methods, people's perceptions of wellbeing and illbeing are described in terms of four dimensions, dimensions that are all relevant to the social settings of our fieldwork too (Laderchi 2001:10)[3].

The first dimension has to do with *material wellbeing*; "lack of food, shelter, clothing, poor housing and uncertain livelihood sources", and in some countries also "having enough to eat all year around..... possession of assets". Uncertain sources of livelihood is an element that is repeatedly mentioned by our informants. For instance in Katharagama, we saw how every source of income was uncertain;

agricultural cultivation, gem mining, and income from pilgrims visiting the sacred town. Coping with the uncertain is an aspect of everyday life, at least all over the dry zone (cf. Baker 1997). The poor condition of housing is another aspect that influences the life of poor people we met during this study. This goes particularly for the estate workers in the 'line houses', and the internally displaced in Puttalam and in Vavuniya.

The second dimension is *physical wellbeing*: "Mainly described in terms of health, strength and appearance", seen as both important in themselves and as preconditions for work. In our study we saw that the health situation of the children is a problem in many of the social settings. This was particularly striking in the Muslim community of displaced persons.

The third dimension is *security*: "Peace of mind and confidence in survival........not just in terms of livelihoods, but also in terms of sheer survival in the face of rising corruption, crime, violence, lack of protection from police and absence of recourse to justice, wars between ethnic groups, tribes and clans, frequency of natural disasters and uncertainties of season and climate".

Related to the situation in the social settings that we studied, the most striking indicator connected to this dimension is the number of women and children who are victims of gender based and intra-family violence. As we have documented, such violence is common, and it is accepted. It also appears that the battered women cannot expect much protection from the police.

Other threats to security are the existence of corruption and crime, particularly in the urban slum, and frequency of drought and flood in the rural dry zone.

This dimension also includes *freedom of choice and action*: "It means the power to avoid the exploitation, the rudeness and otherwise humiliating treatment so often meted out towards the poor by the rich or the more powerful in society. It also includes the ability to acquire skills, education, loans, information, services and resources; to live in "good places", to withstand sudden and seasonal stresses and shocks and not slip further into poverty".

This poverty dimension is particularly relevant for the communities of displaced persons. In the Tamil community in Vavuniya, we found that people had very little expectations in life. They do not have any urge to buy or make new or definitive structures. It is a feeling of transition. This is evident from the utensils they use or even their clothes. The natives too are not immune to this feeling. Living with relocated settlers in close proximity to the 'frontlines', they share the feelings of insecurity and the possible threat of displacement themselves. The field assistant concluded that the villagers seemed to have lost hope in tomorrow.

The impression of apathy was even more striking among the displaced Muslim population who lived in a village which is poor in almost every sense of the word. The marked overall apathy, indifference and despair in the community as a whole alternates with fatalistic acceptance. The lack of leadership throughout the community is striking, and so is the lack of self-esteem. They were displaced more than twelve full years ago and the scars of that event should at least have begun to heal. One may have expected some resilience and vigour in attempting to create a new life for themselves. But all that could be felt was a sense of drift and indifference. There was in addition a helplessness characterised by the endless expectation of outside help to fulfil their requirements.

Acceptance of the displacement is not the big problem. The vast majority have accepted the fact they are unlikely to go back to their native land and even if they did, that they'd need to start again from scratch. The Muslims group reported having gone back using the current ceasefire to find not even the bricks of their own houses, and in their place outsiders (Tamils) having taken up residence in their compounds. The areas to which our study was limited did not allow us to examine the perspective of the Tamil population in these settings.

The last dimension of poverty mentioned in the study based on participatory methods, is *social wellbeing*: "Defined as good relations within the family and the community". All the dimensions described above too can, of course, also be seen as aspects of social well being. Neither the beaten wife, nor the depressed internally displaced person, would secure a high score on a scale of social wellbeing. However, we highlight below two specific elements which are parts of the normative structure in most of our social settings, and which greatly influence the wellbeing of the poor. One element is envy and jealousy, and the other is the active obstruction of others' development.

5.2.2 Envy and jealousy

The desire to prevent others in one's community from overtaking the rest is a recurrent theme. All of the field assistants have, at one time or another, reported that there is an overpowering ethos of 'We must all be at one level' or perhaps even more 'Nobody should improve their living circumstances from their present level'.

What we found is that this is not just a private displeasure at anybody in the community trying to grow or develop beyond the level at which they now operate. It is a more public and shared resentment at whoever dares to leave the others behind. Thus 'jealousy' is shared and used to create a bad feeling about whoever may be suspected of being likely to acquire something better than what the others have.

5.2.3 Active obstruction of others' development

The feeling of 'jealousy' makes people want to keep others down or prevent them from zooming higher, leaving the neighbours behind. Such people therefore have to be prevented from going higher than the level of the rest of the community. The first step in this is to brand them as anti-social or anti-fun or selfish misers. The automatic next step is to label them as proud and hostile – which opens the door to hostility in return. It is easy to do something to bring them back down when they are seen in this way.

One way of keeping others down, that we heard during our study, is to 'borrow' or ask for contributions continually from those who are believed to be prospering. This can be on behalf of those in need or for community development activities. The undertone that the prosperous must not go up too far is almost an unstated message.

Alcohol allows, more than anything else, the least developed members of a group to restrain others from moving up and leaving them behind. This role of alcohol must be noted by anybody interested in working for community development in the kinds of settings that we have described. We saw numerous examples of how people are forced or coerced, with no physical aggression being needed, to contribute to drinking parties, for instance. These parties are not rare events in the most deprived settings. This is one route through which alcohol facilitates the interference with the progress of members of the community. We described elsewhere how these expenditures are never taken into account in any analysis of alcohol expenditures.

A second mechanism too was noticed. This was the use of the freedom that alcohol use offers the user, to dictate to others what they should do. Some people whom the rest want to keep down, do not join in the drinking sessions, but they can still be reached with requests for contributions for other things. An example is simply the request of a loan by someone in distress or a contribution to a communal activity or celebration. If people do not contribute to a common cause (even one that has been invented deliberately to collect money from them) they can be openly criticized and attacked in the drinking milieu. Or they can be loudly abused for their miserliness or pride by someone who is 'drunk'. People then learn to conform, which ensures that they are prevented from advancing economically.

This may be why those who have improved in living status whilst still residing in the overcrowded setting have usually done so because they have had extra power or sponsorship. That has probably helped them resist these demands from the local thugs.

The obstruction of any members of the community overtaking the others and forging ahead is facilitated by what we referred to as the 'porosity' of the living circumstances of the urban poor. The lack of individual and family space, where others cannot intrude, ensures that any slight improvement in economic circumstances is instantly noticed. Appropriate action will then definitely be taken by those who notice the improvement.

The question arises as to whether this finding is an artefact, not really a reflection of reality. The reality that we have described is not a pleasant sight, almost a caricature. People are portrayed as envious, jealous, intolerant and interfering. The interference appears to be with the deliberate aim of ensuring that a family that seems even likely to get ahead is actively undermined. In overcrowded urban settings they are able to do this more easily because they have direct access to what happens in each others' homes.

The picture that emerges is one of nastiness and a deliberate communal complicity to keep everybody down to the level of the others. Is this picture false? We have to examine whether bias in reporting or recording is responsible for creating a false impression. And having re-examined our reports from this standpoint, we still feel that the image that

Conclusions

we portrayed is accurate. The image of viciousness that underlies this image is unlikely, we concluded, to be due to significant bias in the perception of those gathering the data or in the rest of us. The tendency is reported by every field assistant deployed in Colombo, and their reporting was independent of each other.

Conclusion: Those undertaking development work in a 'slum' community, or any other perhaps, must take note of this tendency – that of people working vigorously to keep others from progressing. It is pervasive and significant – and unlikely to be a misinterpretation of the reality that exists.

To develop, individuals and families will have to learn how to insulate themselves from the others who wish to drag them back down. One solution is to move away from or escape from this setting. Nearly all our informants said this was the only way to progress in life.

A strategy for development agencies to follow is to work primarily for collective improvement. This means that they should spend more energy to engage those least able to envisage an improvement in their lives. These persons will likely be the most active agents in undermining the progress of the community as a whole. Engaging them will require new approaches too, as they will likely be the most difficult to engage.

This is clearly a difficult task. A largish community of some size may not be feasible to 'collectively improve', but the strategy of not leaving anybody behind is worth exploring or testing out.

Poverty versus low income

The short vignette that we had about the cooperative shop illustrated that some people whose income was clearly less then that of others were still not as 'poor' as them. The low-income earners in the shop were different from the more obviously poor and deprived groups described elsewhere. There were people in the shop whose earnings were much less than that of the poorer families of the overcrowded urban community, for instance, but they appeared to be less abjectly poor. The contrast with people from the three-wheeler stand was even more stark. The three-wheeler drivers, who appeared clearly less well off than the low income earners in the shop, probably earned several times their income.

What are the differences that may account for the low income earners in the shop appearing to be better off than other low income earners of the overcrowded urban setting or three-wheeler stand? This is despite the fact that the low income earners in the shop received a much lower income than those in the three wheeler business.

We are talking here about few people, less than ten. They may be atypical. If they are not, there are several possibilities underlying this evident difference. One possibility is that the few persons concerned were coincidentally from families that were relatively better off. Another is that getting a monthly salary is somehow more protective than a higher average income earned on a daily basis. The monthly salary is fixed and guaranteed, and so allows planning..

There were other features too of the low-income earners in the shop. They did not live in overcrowded tenements. And their role models came from among slightly wealthier persons working in the same shop. They had to conform to standards of the 'middle classes'. It is probable that they identified with dreams and aspirations of the middle class office mates.

Even the alcohol use and alcohol related behaviour of the middle classes was different. They were not permitted, as much as the others in some of the other settings, to break certain norms of 'decency' even when intoxicated. Physical violence or threats were hardly seen. People were less tyrannized by the verbal as well as physical aggression permitted with intoxication in the other setting. Dominance was not based as much on physical strength or threat. It was more based on a 'office hierarchy', which works on different rules, and at the top of the hierarchy was a woman.

Central to the less evident poverty in the shop may still be the very much lower consumption of alcohol. Alcohol is a topic of conversation more than it is an aspect of day-to-day behaviour. The heaviest drinker is the least dominant here. Tobacco and other drug use too was visibly less in this setting.

We assume here that the low-income earners of the shop did not have a 'side income', for example by stealing from the shop. It is possible that those in the shop were leading less deprived lives because their visible income was supplemented by illegal sources. Our feeling is that this alone is not an adequate explanation. In the three-wheeler stand and among those loitering at Pettah at night we encountered people who were earning much money illegally or unofficially. But the culture to which they belonged ensured that such earnings were immediately spent on the others –mostly for alcohol.

Conclusion: Belonging to the middle class or identifying with its norms and aspirations seems to override low income as a determinant of 'poverty', and the extent and role of alcohol use, as well as behaviour related to use or intoxication, is very different in these worlds. Both of these findings can be used as a basis for interventions, to test whether they can enhance development work.

Potential for change

We found much problematic behaviour related to alcohol use. This calls for responses to address such behaviour. There is evidence from our findings of potential for changing such problem behaviour. We found an enormous range of 'alcohol-induced' behaviours in the different settings. Major differences in reported alcohol-induced behaviour across settings indicate that there is scope for change in such behaviours too, by changing *social responses* to such behaviour. There is no fixed set of behaviours that invariably accompany alcohol use or intoxication across settings.

Patrons of a hotel from different social backgrounds consume the same amount of alcohol at a restaurant, but show very different behaviours, sitting side by side. The 'less sophisticated' group shows much greater loss of inhibitions than the wealthier and 'more sophisticated'. Even the 'less sophisticated' patrons who get boisterous after consuming alcohol elsewhere do not become violent or aggressive in this setting. They only become 'slightly disinhibited'. This hotel is at a slightly higher status than their usual settings and they somehow do not display the common tendency they have of becoming abusive after similar amounts of alcohol used in other settings.

Similar changes were reported at Galle Face Green after alcohol use there was prohibited. Some years ago there were frequent and regular fights and brawls, because groups would consume alcohol and then become aggressive for the slightest provocation. After the authorities prohibited the consumption of alcohol on the green, many people still continued to consume alcohol surreptitiously. Although they drank alcohol now too (some of them until they were unsteady on their feet) the brawls and aggression stopped.

Conclusion: Given the evident 'plasticity' of so-called alcohol-induced behaviour, it should be possible to modify the most troublesome of these behaviours by changing the way people react to such behaviour.

Alcohol, poverty and development

5.5.1 Ambiguous norms

The norms about alcohol use and intoxication are ambiguous. This goes for both major drinking situations, the illicit alcohol that is consumed daily, more or less secretly, and the alcohol, legal and illicit, that is an important element of special festive occasions. Most villagers generally looked down upon those who spent their money on kasippu and who were considered a nuisance to their fellow villagers. Our impression is that the contempt is connected to the drink itself, and not so much to the intoxication. It is not so much of a shame to be drunk, but it is a shame to drink kasippu. For the kasippu drinkers, the state of drunkenness seems to give them a sense of freedom to express themselves, to show a masculine identity and to escape from what may be felt as the hopelessness and powerlessness of everyday life in the village.

Finding better and more rational ways of expressing the same attitudes may be helpful in preventing this kind of drinking. Another disincentive to such consumption would be the evident social norms that are already there about the foolishness of this kind of consumption. These norms are expressed in rather a moralistic way, a way that for some men may invite rebellion.

Ambiguous norms are not the only finding. There is ambivalence too, especially about how to respond to the kasippu trade. Most villagers say they don't want this trade to continue. But they do not want to go against it either. One important reason that the villagers do not go against the kasippu business, is that there are strong economical and political interests involved. We were told that it could be both unpleasant and dangerous to speak directly to the producers and the sellers about the ill effects of their business.

What makes it particularly difficult to confront this problem, is that the business is seen to be protected by the politicians and the police. We were told that when the kasippu sellers fall in trouble they talk to the people in top places and get things sorted out. Several villagers had observed that even though the police raid the kasippu outlets, the business continues. And the accusations against the politicians were rather direct. This makes it hard for the villagers to react.

One element in a prevention strategy would be to put this on the political agenda, and to make it harder for the politicians to continue their support of the illegal alcohol business. There appeared to be no doubt that the availability of the kasippu was considered an important contributor to making the heaviest drinkers continue drinking.

An important and obvious developmental element would be the empowerment of the women. They are victims of domestic violence and of hard times when their husbands spend their income on alcohol. It also seems that the norms discouraging domestic violence are relatively weak. Even when a drunken husband beats his wife to death, the villagers to some extent seem to accept it and to regard it as an accident that could have been expected.

The regular kasippu drinkers are seen as annoying, their drinking leading to domestic violence and to families falling apart. But the massive alcohol and other expenditures at weddings and other special occasions may be even a bigger drain in pure monetary terms. This is an undoubted and unseen hindrance to the economical development of the village, and it is much more accepted. The consequences of a single such expenditure may often last a lifetime. Is it too easy for the villagers to get large loans, that they cannot ever hope to repay, to finance drinking on such occasions? Regulating the market for loans, would make it harder to end up in a situation where alcohol at a wedding is the basis for prolonged indebtedness and continued misery. But the source of many of these loans are informal and it is advantageous for the persons giving loans on high interest to continue the practice. Other means may need to be sought to help communities collectively curtail this self destructive practice.

One reason that big sums of money are spent on alcohol on such occasions, is the operation of strong norms about show off and keeping up with the neighbours. These norms are at the root of much indebtedness and problems. The norms about alcohol as a necessary element in every celebration, is also present as a tacit understanding – and it certainly makes it easier for the kasippu and other alcohol producers and sellers to improve their business.

Conclusions

5.5.2 The paradoxical role of alcohol in the development process

The role of alcohol consumption in the development process is rather paradoxical or at least confusing. Governments, non-governmental organizations and the public at large all want 'development' and economic improvement. But to many, or maybe most, conspicuous consumption is the visible and ultimate proof of increased prosperity and modernization. Increased alcohol consumption, both in everyday life and on special occasions, has been made an inseparable part of the modernization process and the image of prosperity. To many young men in the villages, to be modern and to be developed, includes drinking beer and arrack, and showing it off. Alcohol and other drugs easily serve as symbolic arenas in which to conduct and express the search for a modern identity.

There is also good reason to believe that this new and modern drinking pattern does not substitute the current patterns of alcohol consumption but adds to it (Skog 1988). Thus the much cheaper kasippu continues to be easily available everywhere and to be consumed as before as well.

Conclusion: To reverse the image of alcohol consumption as a sign of economic development, is a necessary and a demanding task for the different actors in the development process. It is relevant to the main trend in development work in recent years - less focus on service delivery, and more weight on capacity building and the strengthening of civil society. Strengthening civil society includes improving its understanding of unseen undercurrents of 'development'.

Notes

1. It is a also known in the literature on drinking patterns, that men drink to attain a feeling of personal power, cf. for ex. McClelland et al. (1972)

2. According to Room (2002:145) studies in Sri Lanka have documented that alcohol is an important factor in the maintenance of poverty. He cites a WHO-report: "Many families are unable to escape from poverty because of the alcohol and tobacco use of one or more members. Once influenced by alcohol use, poverty itself may be exacerbated by absenteeism, lack of motivation, ill-health and lack of family unit".

3. Her five dimensions are based on a report for the study "Voices of the poor":

Glossary

Some words used in this document are not from the English language. A list of these with their meanings is provided below.

aiya – elder brother. Sometimes used to refer in a slightly respectful way to someone older

boarding – any room or lodging taken for payment

chena – a form of cultivation where a brush or forest area is slashed and then burned after which a crop is sown

devala – a place of worship for various deities

ganja – a form of smoked cannabis leaf

kangani – the person in charge of a group of labourers working in an estate

kasippu – the common form of alcohol illicitly brewed and sold

lamaya – a 'young person'

maldive fish – form of dried fish (originally from the Maldive islands) used as an additive in preparing food

resthouse – usually a government owned residential hotel outside of Colombo which also offers food and drink to non-residential patrons

Rs – shortened form for rupee
Rupee – the Sri Lankan currency. At present (1993) converts at around 100 to the US dollar

Samurdhi – state poverty alleviation scheme which offers a small stipend and basket of commodities to those classified as 'poor'

seettu – an informal scheme where several individuals contribute a sum of money monthly and give the total to each one in turn

Sinhala or Sinhalese – the local language spoken by a majority in our study areas and in Sri Lanka

Tamil – the local language spoken by a minority in our study areas and in Sri Lanka

vadey – a popular fried snack of lentils

yala and maha – two major seasons for cultivating, especially of rice paddy. Corresponds with the monsoon rains

References

Abeysekera, D. (2002): *Internally Displaced in Sri Lanka*. Colombo: FORUT and UNHCR.

Abeyasinghe, R. (2002): *Illicit Alcohol*. Colombo: Vijitha Yapa Publications.

ADIC – FORUT (1999): *Summary of National Level Situation Regarding Alcohol and Other Drugs*.

Baker, V. (1997): *A Sinhalese village in Sri Lanka. Coping with uncertainty*. Forth Worth, Texas: Harcourt Brace College Publishers

Busby, Cecilia (1999): "Agency, Power and Personhood" *Critique of Anthropology*, vol 19 (3), pp. 227-248.

Central Bank of Sri Lanka (1987): *The alleviation of poverty in Sri Lanka*. Colombo: Central Bank of Sri Lanka.

Dale, Reidar (2000): *Organisations and Development*. Thousand Oaks: Sage.

Giddens, Anthony (1984): *The constitution of society*. Cambridge: Polity Press.

Hettige, S.T. (1995): "Integrated Rural Development in the Context of Poverty Alleviation". In: Senaratne, J.L. et al. (eds.): *Integrated Rural Development Programme*. Colombo: Regional Development Division, Ministry of Finance, Planning, Ethnic Affairs and National Integration.

Johnston, G. and Percy-Smith (2003): "In search of social capital". *Policy and Politics*, vol. 31, no. 3, pp. 321-334.

Kliksberg, Bernardo (1997): "Rethinking the State for Social Development"; *The International Journal of Technical Cooperation*. Vol. 15, pp. 145.59.

Laderchi, Caterina Ruggeri (2001): *Participatory methods in the analysis of poverty: a critical review*. QEH Working Paper no. 62. Queen Elizabeth House, Development Studies at Oxford.

Lakshman, W.D. (2000): "A Holistic View of Youth Unemployment in Sri Lanka: An Exploratory Study." Page 57- 88, in: Hettige, S.T. and Mayer, Marcus (eds.): *Sri Lankan Youth*.

Leitan, Tressie (1995): *Women in the fishing industry: Participatory development through co-operatives*. Colombo: Logos publications.

MacAndrew, C. and Edgerton, R. (1969): *Drunken comportment: a social explanation*. Chicago: Aldine.

McClelland, D.C. et al. (1972): *The drinking man*. New York: The Free Press.

Narayan, Deepa; Chambers, Robert; Shah, Meera Kaul and Petesch, Patti (1999): *Global Synthesis. Prepared for the Global Synthesis Workshop: Consultations with the Poor*, World Bank, Washington DC.

Rao, Vijayendra (1997): "Wife-beating in rural South India: A qualitative and econometric analysis." *Social Science and Medicine, vol. 44. no. 8, pp. 1169-1180.*

Room, R. (2001): "Intoxication and bad behaviour: understanding cultural differences in the link". *Social science and medicine*, 53:189-198.

Room, R. et al. (2002): *Alcohol in Developing Societies: A Public Health Approach*. Finnish Foundation for Alcohol Studies in collaboration with The World Health Organisation.

Rossow, Ingeborg (1999): "Alcohol-related violence: The impact of drinking pattern and drinking context. *Addiction,* 91, pp. 1651-1661.

Shephard, Jon M. (1990): *Sociology*. Minneapolis/St. Paul: West Publishing Company.

Skjelmerud, Anne (1999): *"What do you do for life if you don't drink?"* Thesis, Department of sociology, University of Oslo.

Skog, O. J. (1986): "An analysis of divergent trends in alcohol consumption and economic development". *British Journal of Addiction*, 47:83-99.

Sonali, D. (1990) *An Investigation into the incidence and causes of Domestic Violence in Sri Lanka*. Colombo: Women in Need.

Subramania, N. (2001): "For greener pastures". *Frontline*, vol. 18, issue 21.

Van der Laan, Anita (1998): *A Participatory Water Supply Scheme on a Tea Estate in Central Sri Lanka*. The Hague.

Veblen, Thorstein (1953): *The Theory of the Leisure Class. An Economic Study of Institutions*. New York: Mentor Books. (First edition 1899)

World Health Organization (1992): *Women and substance abuse, country assessment report*. Geneva: WHO.

Yapa, Laxman (1998): "The poverty discourse and the poor in Sri Lanka". *Transcriptions from the Institute of British Geographers,* Vol. 23, pp. 95-115.